Up In The Sky

h. e. l. i. c. o. p. t. e. r stories

NITIN SATHE

Vitasta

Published by
Renu Kaul Verma
Vitasta Publishing Pvt Ltd
2/15, Ansari Road, Daryaganj
New Delhi – 110 002
info@vitastapublishing.com

ISBN 978-93-86473-37-0

First Edition 2019
Third Reprint 2025

MRP ₹350

Edited by Ankita Athawale
Sketches by Siddhartha Iyer
Cover and layout by Somesh Kumar Mishra
Printed by Manipal Technologies Limited,
Manipal

Contents

In Gratitude

To the Indian Air Force, that has given me a family of friends, a philosophy of life, pride in my work, trials, tribulations, successes and celebrations—the very memories that make the stories in this book.

To the helicopter, that versatile, wondrous bird that gave me flight and perspective, which fueled my appreciation of people and places and extracted from me my best effort and highest commitment to duty.

To all the colleagues and friends who feature in these stories, this book wouldn't have been possible without the times we spent together. I remember each one of you fondly and if you, like me, relive those days through these pages, it would give me immense pleasure to hear from you.

To the readers of my last two books, for reading them, for reaching out to me with kind words of encouragement and wisdom. You nudged a writer, ever unsure about his next book, to let go of doubt and get to the keyboard.

To all those friends—and I have so many! who had faith in this book of memories even before I did. To those of you who read my earliest and worst drafts and had only constructive advice and unfailing trust to return, never any moment of doubt.

To my niece and editor Ankita Athawale for being my co-pilot in this flight of recollections. Thank you Ankita for taking the controls from time to time, for forcing me, much against my inertia, to recall, reconstruct and rewrite over and over again. Your keen eye and sense of aesthetics gave nuance to my writing and craftsmanship to my words. Oh! the joy of seeing an attachment from you titled, '... Final – Good to Go'!

This book is as much a result of your perseverance as mine.

To Siddhartha whom we fondly call 'Pico Iyer', the talented illustrator and fine young man whose sketches for this book are like the tailwind to an airplane in flight – they give the stories speed and reach. In Pico, my childhood friend Kanan Narayanan's son, I see a bright new generation of young people who follow their passion and target excellence in not one but many fields. Thank you Pico for taking time from your guitar and becoming a part of this book.

To my publisher Renu Kaul Verma and her team at Vitasta Publishing who have affirmed their faith in me a third time.

To family and friends who stand by me in everything I aspire to do. It is because of you that I can take-off, hover and soar. It is for you that I return to land.

The helicopter has been described as an assembly of a million rotating parts, each working in unison, so that the bird can fly. What an apt metaphor for the journey of this book!

Here it is now, ready to take flight.

Air Cmde Nitin Sathe

August 2018

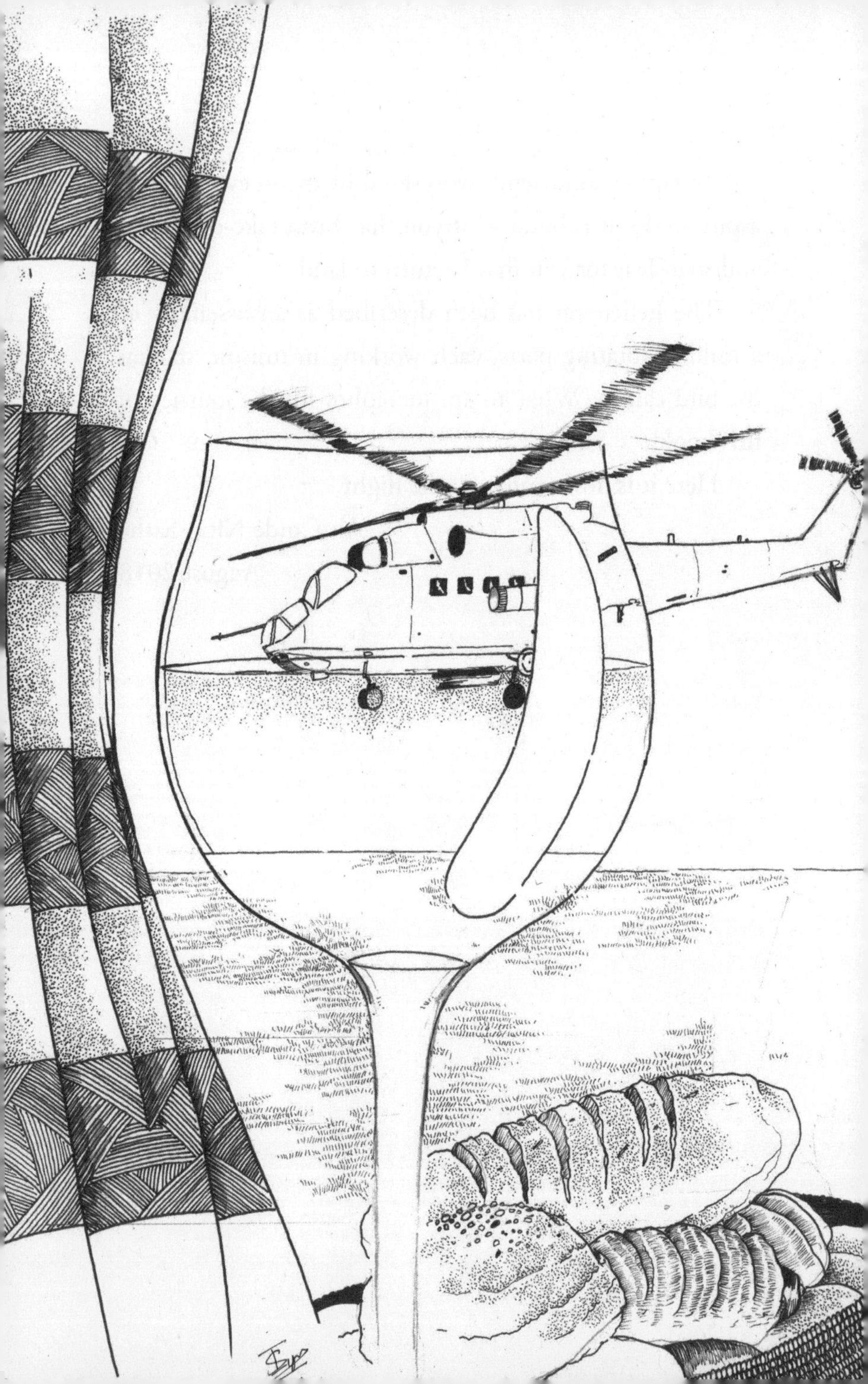

All for a Little Wine

Our unit was to get new helicopters. The helicopters were to come crated from the erstwhile USSR and be assembled in Mumbai before being flown out to our base in the north. The year must have been 1993 because I remember being a young Squadron Leader at the time. I was excited to be detailed to captain the ferrying of one of the gleaming new machines along with co-pilot Flt Lt Ashish Kapoor (Kaps for short) and a flight engineer.

The Russians were already in Mumbai when we arrived at Victoria Terminus one sultry day in the middle of the monsoons. Three crated helicopters had reportedly arrived and been loaded on to big trucks that would transport them to the airport. On the way to the airport, the driver of one of the trucks tried to take a short cut past an over-bridge, as he may have been used to doing often. In this case, he underestimated the height of his cargo and got stuck under the bridge! The result: The main gear box of the new machine was broken and it would be sometime before the machine could be fly-worthy again. Mercifully, the other two crates carrying the helicopters reached the airfield safely. We now hoped that the rest of the mission would be accomplished without a hitch... without any further mishaps.

Within no time, the Ruskis had put the main rotors and the tail portion of the helicopters in place and after a ground check of the engines, they had the machines ready for flight check. When the Russian crew flew together, for emergency purposes, we had an air force controller in the ATC along with an interpreter so that safety was not violated at any time. After the Ruskis were satisfied with the first flight tests on the machines, I was to fly one helicopter along with a Russian pilot for a final acceptance flight. The Russian pilot spoke only Russian but he could understand a very few words of English. In this sortie, I was to fly as an observer and not take to the controls while he demonstrated the airworthiness to me.

Kakaya bcata podnimatcya? – What height to climb to?

Kakoe napravleniye k zemle? – What direction to land?

Razresheniye na bal'et. – Cleared for take off.

Vertolet khorosho? – Is the helicopter ok?

Skorost' is speed, *vysotais* height...such words and simple sentences were written on our thigh pads as a ready reckoner. This is the only and all the Russian I knew. As we lined up on the runway for take-off, Mumbai ATC in his nasal voice instructed, 'Clear for takeoff, maintain takeoff heading and 1000 feet till five nautical miles and then turn left to intercept radial 300 degrees climb to 3000 feet; call 25 miles out for further climb with Mumbai radar'. This had me on the mat. This was beyond my proficiency in Russian and I had to say to ATC, 'Sir I have a Russian pilot on controls who can understand only simple instructions!' There were a few sniggers and giggles on RT after which he did allow us to take off with a simpler set of instructions.

When the aircraft was finally handed over to our all-Indian crew and the acceptance papers signed, we still had to clear other 'running in' tests before we could fly it home to Pathankot. As per safety requirements, it was mandated that the helicopter underwent a check at the end of 5 hours of flying. An endurance flight was also to be carried out to check fuel consumption. Therefore, limited flying time was available to us before the 5-hour check.

Fierce as the monsoons were, we chose Goa as our

destination. We would wait for a suitable clear weather day so that we could sortie without any hindrances. Goa was chosen with another special mission in mind. Our squadron was to have its 10th year anniversary celebrations as soon as we returned with the Russian helicopters. In those days, wine wasn't as freely available outside Goa as it is today. Why not get a few cases of Goan wine to add to the merriment!

Luckily, Mumbai got a break from cloudy weather and we didn't have to wait long before we were on our way to Goa. The flight to Goa was unusually fast because we got a strong tail wind. We were happy that flying hours would now remain well within the 5-hour limit. We also anticipated that the winds would die down by late noon as the weatherman had predicted so that the return journey would not take up the time gained.

When we landed in Goa, many of our brothers from the Naval units showed up to see this new acquisition that they had only read about in the defence magazines. While one of us stayed by the aircraft to look after the refuelling and flight planning, the other crew borrowed a vehicle and drove out of the airfield on the special mission. They came back in a car loaded with crates of wine and packed meals of prawns and fish. The mission accomplished and the aircraft loaded to its maximum, we were soon airborne towards Mumbai.

With the hills of the Western Ghats to the east and with the sun shining over a calm expanse of the ocean to the west, we followed the beaches as we headed north. As the weatherman had predicted, the winds had died down sufficiently. Even so, our progress was not as fast as it was in the morning.

Half way down the route, as we enjoyed the lovely scenery, it started to get dark. Rain clouds loomed ahead. On going closer, we found a thick wall of rain in our path. We quickly decided to fly into the sea and around the bad weather patch. Leaving land behind us, as we descended over the sea, we realised that it wasn't as calm and friendly as it had looked. No sight of land and an air crew without experience in flying over an open ocean made for a rather uncomfortable cockpit. Tense discussions later, we were heading back towards land to try our luck by climbing into the hills and diverting to Pune. As we headed towards the hills, we saw hill tops disappearing beneath thick clouds. It was not worth the risk, we decided. There were two choices in front of us – either divert back to Goa or choose a field nearby and carry out a precautionary landing and wait for the weather to clear.

But we couldn't have made it all the way to Goa either – there wasn't enough fuel. Hobson's Choice – the only land available for landing was right below us.

'Kaps, how do you read?', I asked my co-pilot.

'If we land here we will have to find a suitable place...', he said.

'You look for an appropriate landing field while I try and raise some civil traffic on radio', I said.

'Sir, we have just 700 litres available', Kaps cautioned.

700 litres was just enough for the flying time left to reach Mumbai.

'If we loiter around too much we won't have fuel to reach Mumbai either', I said.

We decided to head along the sandy beaches at low height to determine a suitable landing place.

'I hope we get a good place to stay near the beach', said Kaps to lighten the mood.

'And some good sea food...', I added.

We had to take care to avoid getting into a dust bowl while landing. Beaches have a lot of loose sand flying around as helicopters come to hover. So a green patch near the beach is a more welcome place to land. We also searched for a green patch with a road close by so that help and a refueller could arrive close to the aeroplane.

A little panic had set in by now. Even though we were allowed to do so in extreme circumstances, it was generally a not done thing since it indicated, to some extent, poor planning. Also, landing near a small village on the western coast would make good news for the media besides creating unnecessary ruckus for the local populace. All this flashed through my mind as we prepared for the landing.

'Air Force helicopter flown by Squadron Leader found stranded on beach'. I could imagine the headlines on the photos of us in the local news of the next day.

Once on land, the only option was to switch off and wait for the weather to clear and get airborne, daylight permitting. But we could afford no further landings or diversions after this one since we were critical on fuel. Another landing along the route would mean that we would have to ask for the refuelling vehicles to come on site to give us the much needed juice.

As we reconnoitred the beaches below us, our intercom set decided to quit on us. The spirit of Murphy must have been with us in the cockpit that day, and laughing in glee besides. With a tandem seat helicopter, the only way to communicate now was by pre-briefed signals of motions of the control stick. No amount of shouting could get us to hear each other above the din of the engines and rotors.

Being the captain in command, I took over controls and decided to land facing north on an isolated green field close to the beach. As we came in to land, I saw a small hole appearing in the rain patch ahead and there seemed to be adequate light across it. This was a lucky break, we would be able to cross across to Mumbai now, I thought. I was thrilled to find that my hunch was correct!

As soon as we cleared the rain patch, we could see the Mumbai skyline of Colaba very far into the distance. Suddenly, the intercom came alive too and things started looking not so bleary after all. Murphy had made an exception to the rule and we were silently thankful for this chance. There was a collective sigh of relief from the air crew, now that all was well.

We called up the ATC in Mumbai and established contact, telling them our position and ETA. The ATC controller, in a matter-of-fact tone, informed us that it was raining in Mumbai and since we were flying in visual flight rules, we were not cleared to land. He advised us to either divert to Pune or go back to Goa! This was one of those situations when pilots on their side and air traffic controllers on theirs seriously wonder if the other side is in their right minds! Didn't these guys in civil ATC understand how we operated helicopters? We are not like airliners with tons of spare fuel to divert to other airfields across the country if it was so mandated.

With all the extra time we had spent negotiating the weather, and making decisions about what to do, our fuel tanks were drying up fast. We had to plead with the controller, who reluctantly allowed us over Colaba and asked us to await further instructions. By this time, we were only 10 odd miles from landing. As we reported our position over Colaba, the controller in his stony voice told us to orbit there for about 15 to 20 minutes so as to accommodate some arrivals and departures at the busy airport. I was quite exasperated by then and decided to announce our predicament to the ATC.

'We have just 10 minutes of endurance on board', I told the controller.

There was hushed silence on the other side. A few seconds later, a still stony voice came on again.

'Ok! Roger', he said, giving us priority over the other commercial flights for landing.

How flying makes pilots happy. How the thought of landing on terra firma does too! As we landed I was surprised to see a line of rescue vehicles and an ambulance – to rescue us. We sheepishly called ATC to say that all was under control and we would not require any further assistance.

'Pilots to report to ATC after switch off', said the controller.

I was sure it was for a dressing down and maybe a written explanation. As we taxied to our bay, I decided to switch off one engine to conserve fuel. The warning light indicating low fuel had been already on for more than 10 minutes in the air and I suspected that we had just about 100 odd litres available in the tank. The gauges were not meant to be accurate to show such low levels and rightly so – we were not supposed to land in such a state!

There was a lot of explaining to do to the ATC guys. After many rounds of apologies and thank yous, we were relieved that no official safety violation issues were being raised by them in writing. We hunkered down and discussed where we had gone wrong. When we reached base, we decided to tell our boss all and made sure we shared our experience with all our squadron mates. Many years later, I also wrote about it for the flight safety magazine so that the entire fraternity of pilots could learn from our mistakes.

Squadron spirit, both literally and figuratively, is all right. One need not put the aircraft and its occupants into danger for a few bottles of cheap wine!

Helicopters don't fly, they vibrate so
badly the ground rejects them.
—Tom Clancy

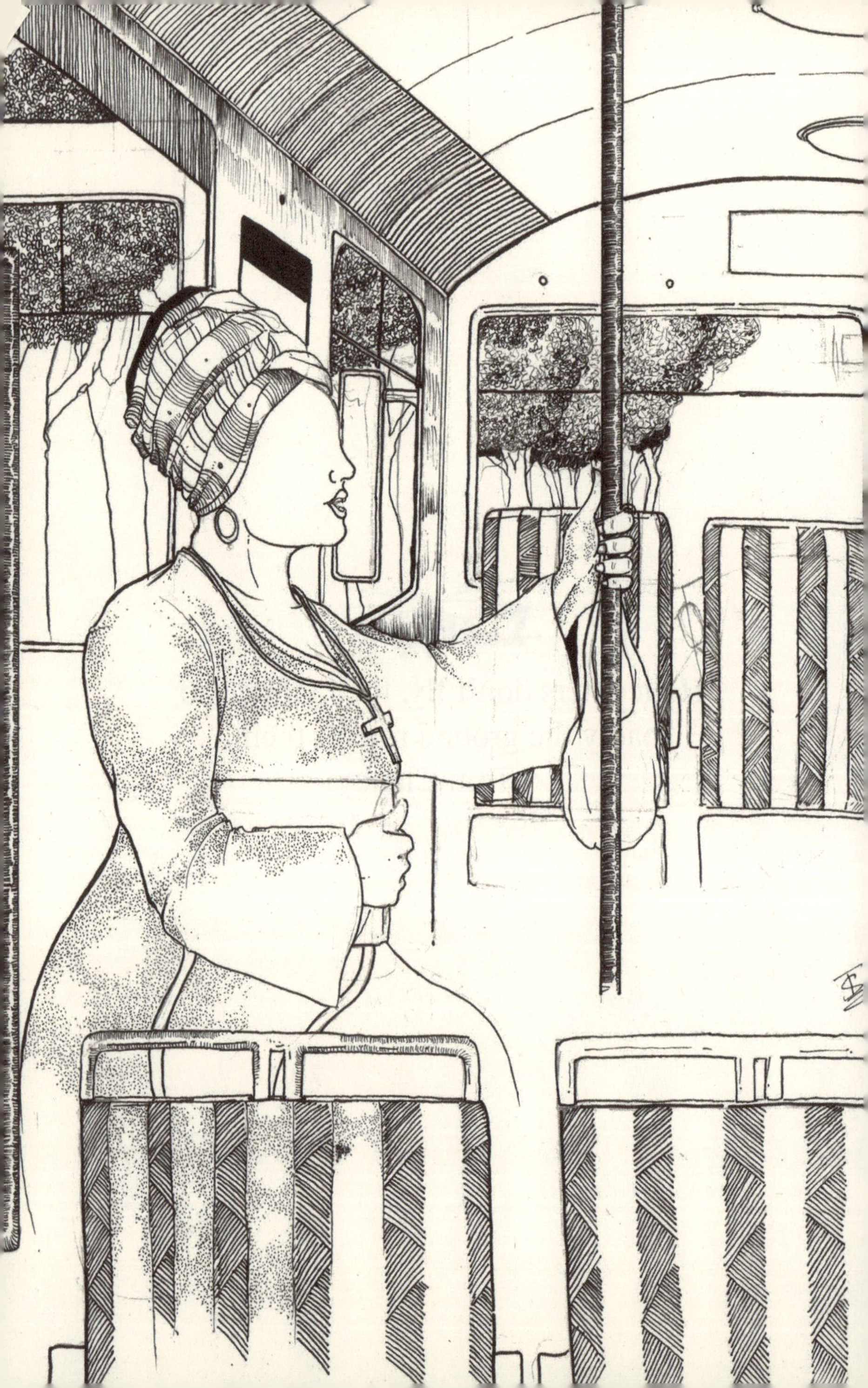

Bus Ride to Nairobi

A large set, middle-aged African woman in a pale beige dress and bright head scarf scrambled on to the bus, a fancy faux leather bag in one hand and a cheap polythene bag in the other. The bus began to move out of the bus station and a plastic water bottle threatened to fall out of her bag as she steadied herself and looked for a seat. There were only a few empty seats and one being next to me, I pushed myself against the window to make place for her. It would have been ideal to have no one on the adjacent seat on an overnight bus ride and I wasn't too pleased for the company when she plonked herself heavily on the seat. A sweet fragrance of flowers permeated the area around and I was glad it wasn't someone smelly and sweaty.

'Hello!', she said brightly, perhaps reading my thoughts, perhaps just being friendly to a foreigner. I was only a few months into my posting at the UN mission in Congo and hearing an English hello on a bus full of people speaking in a tongue I did not understand naturally put me at ease. In return for my polite smile, she smiled widely, revealing a set of perfect pearly whites that shone even more brightly against her deep brown skin tone.

In preparation for a family holiday to Australia, I was on my way from Goma in the Democratic Republic of Congo to Kigali in Rwanda and onwards to Nairobi, the Kenyan capital to apply for a visa at the consulate there. It was the first time that I was undertaking a bus ride off-duty and as the lush, overgrown Rwandan countryside sped past us beneath low, overhanging rain clouds, it seemed to me a fitting metaphor for this beautiful, troubled land long known as the 'heart of darkness' in the 'Dark Continent'. Reminders of strife were everywhere. Equally, there were men in the fields and women with baskets of bananas on their heads going about their quotidian chores like other men and women anywhere in the world.

As I stared out of the window, taking in the ridges and valleys on the outskirts of Kigali, 'It is the city of a million mountains', said the lady next to me.

'My name is Lily', she said, extending her hand towards

me. Usually, I am the one to draw people into conversation, so I was amused by this fellow traveller who seemed more curious about me than I was about her. I told her my name, we shook hands and before we knew it, we had quite forgotten the countryside beyond our window.

One of the first things that Lily asked me was how many children and brothers and sisters I had. It was a strange question but a heart-warming one, for African people, as I found out, have the family foremost in their minds and hearts, just like Indians. And just like Indians, they think nothing of asking a perfect stranger about his or her family. Lily was from Nairobi, she told me, where she lived in a house together with her siblings and their families.

'What do you work in?' I asked her.

'I work with different people from all over', she said.

I thought she hadn't understood and asked again. 'What exactly do you do for a living?'

'I am a ghost writer now. I have been in the media etc. etc., but I am kind of zeroing in on ghostwriting', she said.

'Ghost writing?' I asked.

'I try to help Africans to write. We are great story tellers but very poor at documenting our stories. There are talented writers but they don't know how to publish cheaply etc. etc.', she said.

She used many 'etc. etc.' in her sentences. I wondered

if this meant that there was so much more to be said that it wouldn't fit into a conversation like this or that there was only so much to be said and the etc. etc. served to cushion her work with a sense of magnitude.

'I too have taken to writing. I may get to publish it soon if all goes well', I said. I was at that time compiling my first book on my experiences as part of the Air Force's rebuilding operations in Car Nicobar after the tsunami.

'Good luck with that!', Lily said enthusiastically, smiling widely again. She was liberal with her smiles.

When thc conversation moved to terrorism and war, she spoke of the situation in Africa with neither emotional cynicism nor impractical hope. From the way she spoke of people and politics, she seemed rather well informed and very well connected.

She told me she was doing a book for former president Jerry Rawlings of Ghana. 'All for good will... etc. etc.', she said.

'How long before it is in public domain?' I asked.

'On this continent, trouble subsides in one place only to erupt in another. So who knows?', she said. 'All that energy wasted. Energy that we could have used in nation building.'

'Other than writing work, I go around Africa giving talks on various aspects of life, to get rid of all the ills that ail the continent', Lily declared. I marvelled at her choice of words and her lofty ambition. Maybe it was her faith in Christianity and the long study of its religious texts that made her frame her goals in the absolute. Almost as a messiah would, I thought to myself. Whether she did rid any ills on the continent, I did not know but she seemed supremely confident in her ability to do so.

The setting sun seemed to bring a hush over the chattering crowd in the bus, as if the talkative Africans had tired themselves out and the orange ball of fire going down under the horizon was a sign to quieten down. Indeed, Lily and I too, fell silent and watched the scene. She prayed and crossed herself many times. Some people were bringing out boxes of food, some were dozing fitfully. We passed by a shanty town and a board announced the name which I spelt out….'M..b..a..r..a..r..a'.

'Em barera, with "barcra" pronounced fast in one breath', said Lily.

I earned a pat on my shoulder for getting it right.

'We are in west Uganda now', Lily said. Our bus was going through Rwanda-Uganda and then onwards into Kenya after a brief stopover at Busia – the border check-post between Uganda and Kenya. I told her that I had flown my helicopters from Kampala to Kigali and onwards to the DRC just a few days ago and that I knew the lay of the land from the air.

'It is a beautiful land', she said. 'Only the lucky ones get to see it like you do.'

The bus had stopped on the outskirts of Mbarara now, near a row of street vendors selling a variety of food items. Some passengers got off the bus. Most simply reached out through their windows and bought things to eat. I looked around to see if there was something that wouldn't bother my sensitive stomach. The chicken breast and legs being served hot on a small wooden skewer caught my attention. Unsure, I looked at Lily for approval.

'Don't even look at it!', her raised eyebrow seemed to say. 'You don't know when the bird has been first cooked and how many rounds of heating it has gone through', she said, slipping over her 'r's without pronouncing them in a Kenyan accent that I was beginning to recognise.

There were also bananas on a skewer. They looked alright to me but Lily's disapproving eyes were enough to deter me from experimentation. Seeing others eat around me got my stomach to protest in hunger. I dug into my bag and got out a packet of 'Parle' Glucose biscuits that I had carried as emergency rations. I offered them to Lily and ate my share hungrily. Lily brought out a packet of sandwiches from her plastic bag and offered me some. I was not about to reject the hand of friendship extended to me on a rickety bus on a new continent, neither was I in any mood to resist the lure of a good looking sandwich!

By the time we reached the Kenyan border at Busia, it was a little beyond midnight. We were all asked to leave our belongings in the bus, proceed for immigration and board the bus on the Kenyan side after it had been checked for narcotics and prohibited items. After clearing immigration formalities, while I was waiting for the other passengers to finish, I lit a cigarette. I was walking leisurely toward the bus when a gruff voice stopped me in my tracks.

'Cigaretttte Cigaretttte', said someone behind me. When I turned around, a muscular man loomed up ahead of me like the Giant to Jack on the beanstalk. I looked up and saw his stern face and steely eyes staring me down angrily. Fearing that I was going to be mugged, I looked around for help. But there was no one within earshot.

'Cigaretttte', said the giant thrusting his hands in front of my face. Maybe he just wants a cigarette, I thought to myself.

'Why this cigarette?' I asked. 'I offer you a fresh one. Take as many as you want', I ventured to say, copying his accent so that he could understand. I held out my packet of cigarettes for him.

'No! This one', he protested, asking me to hand over the one in my hands, which had almost burnt itself out anyway.

Having no more patience with my confusion, he pulled the cigarette out of my hands and threw it to the ground, stubbing it with his big boots.

'Come with me', he said and turned towards a hut with a bare bulb shining inside it.

Realising that he was some kind of security person, I was a bit relieved to walk alongside him towards the hut. There, in a scene fit for cinema, I met the giant's boss – a puny man with buck teeth, an antithesis to the giant who had escorted me.

'Pakistani?', he asked.

'Indian', I said, handing over my diplomatic passport. The puny boss now broke into a smile that showed his tobacco stained teeth. I thought of Lily and her smile and had a wild notion of making a dash to the bus and taking my seat next to her. I imagined the bus leaving the Kenyan border and this tobacco stained chap flailing his hands, running after me in a frenzy.

'*Kidhar rehte ho, India me?'* (Where do you stay in India?) The unexpected question in Hindi took me by surprise.

I was still gaping at him wondering if I was expected to answer in Hindi or English when he continued anyway. '*Hamara* country *me*, smoking is not allowed in the open', he went on to explain.

'Very very sorry' I said, feigning ignorance. 'There was no

board around neither was there any public announcement.'

'In normal case, I would have to apprehend you and produce you in front of the magistrate on Monday morning for a fine', he said. 'But since I have studied in an Indian college for a few years, I will pardon you.'

I thanked him, shook hands and turned to leave when he called out to me.

'Sir!', he exclaimed. '*Chai paani ke liye kuch paise dijiye!*' (Give me some money for some tea and snacks.)

He had learnt his lessons in India, hadn't he! At that time though, I couldn't have been more relieved to dig into my pocket for my wallet. Running a quick mental calculation and deciding on a thousand francs, I handed him a currency note. Damages only worth a dollar, I thought to myself and walked away as fast as I could. To my consternation, I realised that the giant was following me to the bus! Now I really wished the bus would be on the road before he got to me. But before I could get on the bus, I was face to face with the giant again.

'Sir asked me to convey thank', he said. 'The amount you gave us will make our families happy.'

I must have looked at him quizzically because he said, 'Ten thousand francs must be equal to my boss's monthly salary'.

From the corner of my eye, I could see Lily waving to

me now, motioning to me that the bus was about to leave.

I smiled at the giant and said, 'Enjoy. And my best wishes to your family'.

Lily was perturbed about my run-in with the authorities. 'Thank the Lord!', she said multiple times after we were on the road again. 'Thank the Lord you weren't stripped of all your belongings', she said.

When the bus got into Nairobi the next morning, the city had already woken up to its daily hustle bustle. Lily offered that I accompany her home to freshen up and get ready for the day. I am glad that I accepted because not only did I get a hot cup of tea, a hearty breakfast but also a precious briefing on how not to get lynched, robbed or arrested in Nairobi.

'Do you have change to pay for the Matatu?', she asked as I finally rose to leave. I showed her my dollar bills.

'A sure shot way of getting robbed! You carry the local currency in coins', she ordered and returned with more than a handful of coins – change enough to get me through local transport in Nairobi for days.

Kissing the cross around her neck, she said to me, 'Life is too short, the world is too big and God's love is too great to live ordinary'.

And then, I was on my way.

We go on about our lives and we imagine that the

people we meet and befriend on our way, go on about their lives too, taking buses and trains, watching the sun shine and the leaves fall, going to work and going home, paying their bills and drinking tea. I never met Lily or spoke to her again after that day. We, however, remained connected on mails and Facebook. And even though I found out that she died of cardiac arrest a few years later, I still think of her as plonking herself on a seat somewhere, wiping her brow and saying Hello! to a stranger on a bus.

Chicken Singh

If he was aware of the terms of endearment by which we, the junior pilots of the squadron addressed him in private, he never let us know. For us, he was Chicken Singh or simply CS. Anyone who knew the Squadron Leader could say with confidence that the two activities that he loved most were chicken eating and helicopter flying. It won't be an exaggeration to say that birds – both the animate and the inanimate kind – were an obsession with Chicken Singh. We had many opportunities to fly together and no one who accompanied him on these missions would deny that he was fun to fly with.

In the monsoon of 1985, Bihar was, not unusually, under a spate of incessant rain. The Ganga had burst across its banks and reached over into areas that men and women had considered their own. Entire villages and fields were under water and families were stranded. The IAF, like every other year, had been called in for the rescue and relief effort.

CS was the leader of this mission. Flying for external agencies came with perks – all expenses paid, stay at five star hotels – and at such times, Chicken Singh was at his best. He would go out of his way to wrangle the best accommodation from the authorities. Although it was required that we be provided with all the facilities by the State government, it was rarc to havc somconc on our side who would demand the same as a matter of right. CS stood his ground for the littlest of comforts for his officers. For himself, he went a step further and 'managed', among other things, extra vehicles for purported liaison trips and he was often seen buzzing off in a flashy hotel car after the day's flying was done.

The first evening, CS ordered everyone to be in his room by 19-30 hrs to discuss the next day's operations over a few drinks. We were hoping that CS had managed a few bottles of whiskey from his contacts in Patna because buying drinks in a five star hotel would have been far too expensive for young *fauji* pilots like us.

On our way to his room that evening, we saw Chicken Singh arguing with the hotel staff.

'Can I not sign for liquor? I am here on duty, you know. All my expenses are paid for', he was saying to the bartender.

'Any aerated drinks or juice may be signed for, Sir. Not liquor. Those are the rules', came the reply.

'What if I sign for juice and you give me liquor in lieu? That should work, no?', said CS, grinning at us widely, as if he had hit upon a solution that no one else had seen.

The bartender, who had been smiling courteously all this while, now began to show the first signs of exasperation. Not one to back down without a bottle or two, Chicken Singh persisted nevertheless. He suggested to the bartender that it was a win-win for both sides.

'The government is willing to spend money on me if I have juice. With the same money, I will just have some whiskey, *yaar*', he explained.

When the bartender finally called upon a senior manager to parry with Chicken Singh, our man must have realised that he wasn't going to have his way. Chicken Singh looked at us and said with a flourish. 'Boys! I don't know about you. I don't feel like drinking today. We take off early tomorrow.'

He then called a waiter and asked for a menu card. After some instructions to the waiter, 'See you in the room', said CS and left in a jaunty stride. All our crew trooped up to his room, feeling a little downcast about having to attend a briefing without the drinks.

As we were going up the stairs, the smell of *tandoori* chicken seemed to join us and follow us all the way to the third floor. Another 'crew' – that of the hotel's room service – joined us. They followed us to CS' room and before we could settle down, they had laid out an array of snacks on the table. More plates full of chicken snacks were lined up on window ledges.

Some of us recognised a few items as ones we had never ordered out of concern for the right hand side of the menu. Even though drinks were in short supply, the chicken was more than we could eat. The thought of not being able to consume all the food on the table was one that seldom crossed our young minds until that evening. The vegetarians among us joked about the number of chicken who had laid down their lives for Chicken Singh. The evening continued with no reference to any 'brief'. *Tandoori* chicken, in large amounts, can be as heady as whiskey, we found out. The operations brief would wait for the next morning.

The next morning found us in the thick of things, the chicken enjoyed and forgotten. Hundreds of food packets were to be dropped and many VIPs taken for aerial reconnaissance. While these operations were always trying and tiring, it was consolation enough to know that we could be of help to many in distress. Post an exhausting day of flying, it was customary to meet up with the boss and have a debrief followed by a drink and in this case, some chicken too. Chicken Singh did not skip his chicken at any meal, come rain, flood or both, as was the case that year.

When the waters receded and the State government declared that they did not need our support any longer, they hosted us for dinner on the final evening before we went back to base. Great things were said about our valuable support to the suffering populace, about how the armed forces could be relied on every time to bring succour in Bihar's flood situations etcetera, etcetera. The press was there and between tearing down chicken legs and smacking his lips over butter chicken, CS made a statement to the press. Our contribution to relief made front page headlines.

With our work done in Patna, it was to be a long haul back to base involving three en-route halts. With the flight plan filed, we waited at the craft, all loaded to go back. But Chicken Singh was missing. He had asked us to get the helicopters ready and he was to join us at the airport after clearing the bills at the hotel. He had stopped to say bye to his friends in town, we were told.

It was getting hot and humid and we were quite drained by the time his jeep arrived. He walked gleefully to the aircraft giving us a thumbs up. Behind him followed a man with a huge plastic packet containing many small cardboard cartons. We could hardly see the man behind the pile of packets. These were soon loaded into the helicopter and we were ready to go. Chicken Singh almost looks like a chicken himself, I thought to myself as I strapped myself in the captain's seat of the second helicopter.

When we landed at the first base for refuelling, we were accosted by the smell of chicken-mixed-turbine-fuel. I don't know if anyone found that particularly inviting but CS invited us proudly and with a wave of his hand said, 'Come guys, you must be hungry. Help yourself to some food!' Food, for CS, meant only one sort of food. The smell of chicken was overwhelming and I, for one, avoided eating anything in the sweltering heat of the afternoon.

Someone took the co-pilot aside and asked him how it was to fly with so many dead birds in the aircraft.

'If I am not a dead bird by the time I get home, I will give thanks to the Lord', he said.

All along en-route, wherever we stopped for fuel, we saw CS with a cardboard box of chicken-something-or-the-other in his hand. In flight, as we flew behind his helicopter, I could swear I could smell the *tandoori* chicken in our cockpit! The heat must have taken its toll on the chicken by the time we landed at base. The smell was overbearing. The co-pilot was heartily congratulated for having endured the olfactory assault from the accompanying chicken and made it out alive.

Before we disbanded, CS made a kind offer to us, 'Whoever wants to take the food home is most welcome to do so.' We ventured to suggest that the chicken may no longer be fit for consumption. But the man wasn't one to be detracted. When none of the others showed interest in the chicken, 'I'll take it then', he said.

Chicken Singh was celebrating his wedding anniversary that evening. The whole unit landed up at his place with cake and the rest of the goodies. Those of us who had returned from Patna especially looked forward to a laid back evening of celebration close to home. When the snacks were served however, all the crew who had gone to Patna must have decided to turn vegetarian for the evening. The other officers and families were impressed with the spread of chicken snacks. I overheard someone saying that the flavour was special, quite 'unlike the usual'!

When we were leaving, I noticed a set of wine glasses on Chicken Singh's bar. At first, I didn't think much of it. It was his anniversary after all. But then, I realised why I had stopped at the wine glasses – they bore the emblem of the hotel in Patna!

Chicken Singh noticed me looking at the glasses and offered an explanation – 'I signed for the chicken and got these in lieu. The catering fellow was very understanding. Not like the bartender', he said.

Outside, the party was in full swing. Many couples were on the dance floor already. Someone announced that the birdie dance would be next. Yes! The birdie dance was a craze in those years and even the hesitant dancers would join in the merriment for this one.

'Come on', said Chicken Singh.

I imagined all the birds so lovingly consumed by Chicken Singh to be looking down from the heavens and having the last laugh on seeing Chicken Singh turn into a birdie with the 'birdie dance'!

If you are in trouble anywhere in the world,
an airplane can fly over and drop flowers,
but a helicopter can land and save your life.
—Igor Sikorsky

Cooking a Surprise

It had been an exhausting month for the station. Everyone had worked hard for the air exercise followed by the mother of all inspections by the team from Delhi. 'Exercise' in *fauji* lingo, is the simulation of war-like situations that test the entire machinery of the station – administration, maintenance, logistics, operations – to make sure it works like a well-oiled unit. Lessons learnt from the exercise go towards capacity and capability building in preparedness for war.

After a hectic month, a hard-won, relaxed weekend was at hand. The married officers were taking time off with their families. As my wife hadn't joined me in this posting and even though I was the station commander, I was practically part of the bachelors' crowd. They often invited me to their parties and made me feel part of their gang. It was great to be part of an enthusiastic young bunch again. I also welcomed it as an opportunity for me to mingle with the young blood of the station and get a sense of their morale and their concerns. While the youngest are often pushed to work the hardest, they also need special encouragement and support to help them stay motivated and committed while they adjust to the tough demands of their new jobs. After all they were at the end of the food chain and the buck literally stopped at them!

As we wrapped up the inspection on Friday afternoon, a plan was forming in my head. When Saturday came, it was time to follow through on the plan with action.

The large *peepal* tree behind the house would be the perfect setting for my surprise. I decided to have a few charpoys and some Indian style seating on mats and cushions on the ground. My resourceful helpers managed to find some push-carts of the kind used by local vegetable sellers in the village outside the cantonment. These were rolled in from the back gate and placed some distance away from the seating area. These would serve as stalls for food. A sound system and some selected music were tucked away in an enclosure near the boundary wall. Earthen pots that would hold the welcome cocktail were stacked at the entry pathway to my home.

I was going the whole hog. I got a hole dug in the ground and a temporary wood fire *chulha* made for the cooking of *biriyani*. On Friday evening, I had gone to the bazaar, chosen the best cuts of meat and marinated it with generous quantities of rum, curds, herbs and spices. As per tradition, *biriyani* is meant to be cooked over a slow wood fire. When the meat and rice is almost done, a glowing ember of wood is taken out of the fire and put inside a steel vessel over which a generous amount of *ghee* is poured. This smoking vessel is kept inside the cauldron that holds the *biriyani* and the entire thing is sealed. Food enthusiasts like me swear by the authenticity of a *biriyani* cooked in this way; its delicate flavours and distinct smoky taste is no match for the quick and easy meat and rice jumble cooked on a gas stove and passed off as *biriyani*.

So I spent a lovely Saturday afternoon sipping chilled beer and replicating this intricate process of *biriyani* making in my backyard. The layering of rice and meat, the sealing of the pot, the adding of saffron and milk, the sautéing of *kaju* and *kishmish* in pure *ghee* – I wanted to get it all right down to the last detail. Alongside the non-vegetarian *biriyani*, another cauldron with vegetables and paneer in rice simmered away in identical fashion. I was secretly amused by the appreciative looks from my cook when he found out that not he, but I, was going to be cooking.

By early evening, I was itching to reveal the surprise. I only hoped that the youngsters hadn't yet left for an evening out in the city. As if on my evening walk, I stepped out in my running gear and made my way towards the bachelors' living quarters. I found some of them drinking tea and chatting outside their rooms. My appearance made a few run for cover since they weren't properly attired, not in the *fauji* sense of 'proper'.

I pretended to have stopped by to say hello.

'What plans for the evening?' I asked them.

I was relieved to hear a few tentative responses but no big plans.

'How about offering me a cup of tea?' I asked. Someone ran in and got me tea in a glass.

'Don't you have decent cups and saucers in which to offer tea to your guests? And the bloody taste of smelly flasks hasn't left our tea in the 28 years that I have been in service!' I scolded.

A long-winded lecture followed. I enjoyed lecturing them on how little things of presentation – such things as a good cup of tea in a respectable cup – were integral to officer-ly life. This evening, I laboured over it even more as they nodded their heads at everything I had to say. Seniors have all been youngsters once and I knew that behind their respectful looks of compliance, there was grave boredom at my unusually long lecture. They didn't guess it at the time but it was all part of my surprise for them.

'How many of you go for a run?' I continued.

Only a few hands went up. 'Oh!' I exclaimed a tad too dramatically and I thought I had given myself away there. I plunged into another monologue on the importance of fitness in uniform.

'What better time to start than now!' I declared. Then I ordered everyone to get into PT rig in half an hour and proposed that we get together for some running around the airfield. By this time I had to control my urge to laugh out loud at the incredulous faces that looked back at me. They couldn't believe I could be ruining their first relaxed weekend after a month. Unfair! That's what each of them was thinking no doubt but the poor folks couldn't get themselves to say it to my face. Returning after exactly half an hour, I found a hapless bunch of people in PT whites waiting for me.

'I have had a change of mind', I told them. 'Get dressed in jazz rig and meet me outside my house in thirty minutes.'

This time there were a few smiles in the group. Some people had seen the cat peeping out of the bag and others were as perplexed as ever.

'Oh and if you don't know what a jazz rig is, find out from each other', I said, still keeping up my act.

By the time a colourful group in flashy clothes and funny headgear arrived at my gates, the act was off and the surprise was thrown open. The party was on. I was happy to see their smiles and open laughter. They took over from here. Someone managed the music. Another took over the service of snacks. Snack and drinks went around and around and were consumed at an astonishing pace. The Indian themed party was an instant hit because it was different from the standard *fauji* parties. It allowed everyone to lounge and relax without caring so much for *fauji* protocol as in the more formal parties. It turned out to be just the kind of evening I had envisioned. One of the youngsters termed it the let-your-hair-down party of the year. I found some guys on top of my official vehicle parked in the porch. They were enjoying a drink on the bonnet! I had to politely but firmly ask them to show due respect for the official vehicle and step down to enjoy their drink elsewhere. Some people had clearly taken the let-your-hair-down party too far.

After the dessert was served, people went to the cook to thank him for the food. When they were told that I had cooked for them, their jaws dropped and the happiness quotient went up a few notches – both theirs and mine. So happy were they that they went about clearing my fridge and bar of all that was interesting to eat and drink, especially the chocolates and the wine!

As I hit the sack that night, the words of my flight commander from my younger days came to mind – 'A commander must develop multiple personalities', he would say. 'At work and in the cockpit one must demand competence, not tolerate any nonsense. At home and on the social front, a commander must be a big brother sometimes, at other times a parent....'

To mingle with the group that you lead so that they think of you as one of them but also allow them space enough to thrive and grow independently – that is the enduring challenge of leadership. In the end, the mantra is simple: The best workplaces are made of happy people and happy people make people happy. It sure makes me happy to make people happy!

HARIDWAR

Friends on a Train

It is not every day that you hear melodious singing live on a train. So when I did, I was curious to locate the voice and the singer. We were on the Shatabdi Express from Delhi to Dehradun. It has an all chair-car seating and it turned out the singer was in the seat behind me. I remember my first impressions of her – about 60 years old, fair and curly haired with eyes that seemed to hide nothing.

It was to be a short journey and I had cosied myself to a Ruskin Bond novel. Whether it was my curiosity or her voice rising above that of the train, I couldn't help hearing the conversation she was having with the young girl sitting beside her. It was clear from her accent that she was from one of the southern States of India. She was telling the young girl about wanting to see all the important shrines in India before age caught up with her.

For those with a curiosity about new people, having a talkative person sitting behind you in a chair car is all you need for a memorable journey! As the train made its first short halt, I overheard her complaining about her cell-phone and her distress at not being able to call home.

'May I have a look ma'am?', my officer-like qualities came to the fore. 'You could use my phone to call, if you like', I said.

Hesitant at first, she took up my offer and made a short call in Telugu.

When she returned my phone, I introduced myself. 'Nitin Sathe with the IAF in Dehradun.'

'I am Chandralekha', came the reply. The name suited her just fine, I thought to myself.

'Nice to meet you', I said. It was one of those times when the common social exchange was exceptionally heartfelt. Something about this sprightly old lady on a solo trip to the shrines of North India endeared itself to me. I had to turn around in my seat to speak with her as the conversation warmed up. Sensing my agony or possibly annoyed at her forced inclusion in our conversation, the girl next to Chandralekha offered to exchange seats with me. While the girl could catch a nap, it saved me a crick in the neck!

We continued talking. I did what I could to get the mobile going. I handed it over to her with the 'I did it' look and she smiled. As she tried to call, the thing went kaput again. My technological victory was short-lived but I was beginning to make a new friend nevertheless.

'What do you do for a living?', I asked her. Sensing that it may be the wrong question considering her age, I quickly corrected myself to frame the question in past tense.

She said she had worked in a public sector company as a HR manager and thereafter with a multinational as the head of HR. I had recently become involved in the HR function of the IAF and we got around to speaking about nuances and theories of HR. She went on to tell me about the concept of lean management, a new buzz word in the field of HR. I realised that the IAF had been practising lean management for many years without calling it so. I made a mental note to go back and speak to my officers about it.

After an active life in a demanding job, she had retired and now pursuing her hobbies and heart. She always wanted to visit all the 113 '*Dhams*' or religious shrines of importance, she told me. She was planning on going on the Mansarovar *yatra* the next year, she added. I told her that I had flown in the area and seen it from far-from-the-air.

'Travelling alone in India – that too by rail!' I exclaimed.

'Why not?', she said. 'It is quite safe, isn't it?' she asked naively.

'I am quite impressed by your adventurous spirit and determination', I lauded her.

Like a young lad wanting to impress, I told her that I was writing a book on the Tsunami which had been the most adventurous experience for me so far. She asked me many questions about it and almost matched my own enthusiasm for the book! Haridwar was fast approaching. She did not seem too perturbed that her mobile phone was faulty and said that she would show it to some local vendor there. I advised her that there may not be adequate expertise available at Haridwar.

'I suggest you take my mobile and put your sim-card in it', I said. Carrying two mobile handsets, considered overkill on most occasions, comes to use sometimes. I assured her that I did not have use for the other one and that she did not need to return it in a hurry. Politely refusing, she said that she would use the pay phones or simply borrow a mobile in case it was required.

'How are you planning to travel from Haridwar upwards into the hills?', I asked her.

'Just look around for families or groups travelling in that direction and choose my company', she said with a twinkle.

So much for her confidence in the goodness of people!

The train was slowing down, her destination a few

minutes away now. It was time to exchange numbers and contact details and say our goodbyes.

'Would you like to travel by helicopter to the shrine?' I asked her just as the train was entering the platform at Haridwar.

I would have expected her to be surprised. Without batting an eyelid, she said, 'Why not! I would save a lot of time and energy that way.'

Quickly, I scribbled the numbers of my pilot friends who flew helicopters in that area and bid farewell to her. It was now a matter of my reputation to ensure that she got a helicopter ride. I made a call or two to my friends and was relieved to know that they were at Haridwar as we spoke. They assured me of help to the lady.

A little while later I was surprised by a message from Chandralekha. 'Mobile repaired by roadside vendor. Boarded jeep with family of five. On way to Guptkashi. Hope to find friend + helicopter there! Thank you, regards!'

I smiled at her cryptic style. Very military like.

By the time the train got to Dehradun, the journey was forgotten and I got back to the grind. A few days later, I received another message from Chandralekha.

'Helicopter ride fantastic. Thank you thank you! Haridwar now. Now to Pathankot and onward to Jwalamukhi. Any contacts there?'

She really was something. With the time gained due to the helicopter ride, she had plotted out another shrine to visit. I rang her up. It was good to speak with her again.

'Jwalamukhi is a good 150 odd kilometres from Pathankot', I told her. 'What time are you landing up there and how do you plan to go?'

'Reaching around midnight and if I can, I will take a taxi immediately to Jwalamukhi', she said.

I admired her spirit but I wondered if she was being too carefree.

'No way! Do not even venture out of the railway station till daybreak. Let me see what can be done', I said.

After a quick call to my friends in the Air Force station there, I called her to say that a room had been arranged for her at the mess.

'You will be received at the station by an IAF policeman. I have asked them to book a taxi for you in the morning. Have a happy journey.'

I wondered why I was going out of my way to help an unknown person. I guess the only answer to that is that it was because it made me happy. Why do we do anything after all if it isn't to make our own lives pleasanter?

The next time, I was expecting her message before I received it. She was off to Jammu to visit the Vaishno Devi shrine. She asked for my support as if she had known me for years and I responded as if it was my duty to help her. Blessing me profusely and thanking me, she hung up. That was all I needed.

We lost touch after this. I wondered how her trip to Jammu had been. My messages to her remained undelivered. I thought her mobile had given up on her again and hoped that she had reached the safety of home down south. Meanwhile, I got busy with work and Chandralekha slipped quietly into the background.

One day, a couple of weeks later, I received her call as I got home from work.

'I am in Bangalore safe and sound', she sounded happy. 'You know what? From Jammu I decided to travel to Srinagar. At the airport I was told that there was a flood like situation at Srinagar due to incessant rains for the past few days but I decided to press on.'

'How did you manage there?' I asked.

'Oh, that's another long story!' she exclaimed. 'On my flight I was sitting with another kind hearted gentleman who was in the business of selling Kashmiri silk sarees and cloth material in mainland India.'

'As kind hearted as you', she said. I marvelled at how she met kind hearted people everywhere she went. I wonder if in that moment, jealousy crossed my mind for a flash before I brushed it away. The other kind hearted gentleman had taken her to his home on the outskirts of Srinagar which was not so badly affected by the floods. Here she had stayed with his family who had taken a liking to her and adopted her for a week until the waters subsided.

'I started this journey with you so many days ago', she continued. 'It is thanks to you that my trip has been so thrilling and complete', she said and signed off.

In the months that followed, I got busy with my own life and once in a while, I wondered where she was, whether she was in India or at some shrine in another country. Something told me that I would hear from her sooner or later. I wasn't expecting it from a strange, unknown number though.

'Congratulations on the book release', she surprised me. 'I have ordered my copy and I'll need the author's signature the next time we meet', she said. She had been tracking the release and reception of my book on the tsunami.

We 'meet' so many people in life but we only become friends with a few. Maybe friendships, like marriages, are made in heaven. Something draws two people together in a friendship and something tells them that even though a journey may be a short one, the friendship is for the long haul. When I decided to write my second book, Chandralekha was one of the first people to read, edit and critique my drafts. She has also made it a point to visit me at every new place of my posting – to visit the shrines in the vicinity. I now call her my FPG – friend, philosopher and guide!

So the moral of this story would be: Always listen to conversation in the seat behind yours. Always offer to help fix mobile phones. Always offer a hand of friendship and it is unlikely that your will not be held by another's. If one is held out to you, don't hold back. There's no telling when a new friend will walk into your life.

Going Solo

Some moments in life are more special than others and then there are a few that make the milestones, those that are imprinted on your memory as benchmarks of the absolute joie de vivre that you are capable of. Most of us look back at our first jobs, first promotions, first pay cheques – our first steps into the world – and liken that lightness of being, that weight of responsibility, that exhilaration in our own abilities to the sense of soaring the skies. And so it was with my first solo flight. Only that taking off on one's own, taking the controls, steering through bad weather and manoeuvring a safe landing all become quite literal in the life of a pilot!

I graduated from the National Defence Academy

(NDA) in the winter of 1983 and after a month of well deserved rest, reported for flying training at the Air Force Academy (AFA) at Hyderabad. From riding around the NDA campus on bicycles, we were soon going to be flying aeroplanes. It was called graduating – from bikes to jets.

Alas. We weren't going to be flying as early as we had thought. For weeks, we didn't get anywhere near an aircraft. There were checks and emergencies to be mugged up, procedures to be understood and ground tests to be cleared before one could really fly.

I had dreamt of flying for as long as I could remember. Although my father, an army man to the core would have loved it if I had joined the Army like him, I had different ideas. I remember the first time we saw a flying machine, we were at Devlali in Maharashtra where my father was posted. I was all of seven and starry eyed when I was taken to see the small army observation aeroplanes and helicopters at next door Nasik where they were located. It was my father's friend 'Rege uncle' who showed us around and made us sit in the cockpit. On hindsight, I think that the seed of flying was sown there. Later, I remember Rege uncle flying over our house and dropping some chocolates for us from his helicopter. And I used to dream of being up there and doing the same for my friends. The first time I flew in an aeroplane was when I was in eighth grade in Delhi. We were taken to Agra for a day's trip by the only airline available in those times, Indian Airlines. I also remember that my father had to pay a princely sum of 90 rupees for the ticket! In the aeroplane, we were allowed to have a quick glimpse of the cockpit as we went to sit in our seats. And when we took off, there were butterflies in my stomach and a twinge to fly the machine myself! The same feeling I encountered a few years later.... Now that I was so close to being allowed free reign of an airplane, I doubted if I could really take one into the air by myself, and keep it there! Our instructors at AFA had a tried and tested way of keeping cadets alert and on-edge.

'If you can't pass your solo, you may as well forget about flying. Pack your bags and go home', they would say casually, knowing fully full well that to forget about flying was unthinkable to young men (there were no women cadets in those days) who had dreamt of flying all their lives. It served us well however. And in retrospect, I remember my instructor as a wise and patient man, who taught me to fly, both figuratively and quite literally.

'Look at those villagers down there... they are all running away when you come in to land', he would say, commenting on my flying skills. 'If you aim the aircraft there, you would be landing in one of the homes', he would say... 'and I am sure that they will not welcome you if you barge into their home like this.'

'Treat her like a baby, there... gently does it... and she will behave herself', he would say when we fought with the controls of the aeroplane trying to get it do what we wanted it to do.

In 20 days and 20 sorties on the Kiran, a jet trainer, I had come to rely on my instructor, who had never raised his voice, except when the situation veered towards life threatening! Others, I had heard, had gone through some not so happy experiences with instructors sometimes losing their cool in the cockpit, resorting to shouting and screaming to teach my friends how to fly. I think I was lucky in that aspect.

Before he could clear me for a solo flight, I had to complete a touch-and-go sortie, which meant taking off and landing in a circuit. I hoped for the best conditions – westerly runway, strong winds without crosswinds and my favourite machine registration no 761 to fly on. Pilots, like jockeys, have their favourite beasts – the ones that will be controlled smoothly and do exactly as they are instructed.

As trainee pilots will learn, weather gods respond negatively to unreasonably ardent prayer. On that day, the more I hoped for fair weather, the worse it became. The butterflies in my stomach wouldn't rest until I was over and done with the sortie. At long last, the weather cleared enough to fly, and my check instructor and I were up and away into a cloudy sky. I was told that I was to demonstrate two good landings to qualify for a solo flight.

Trainee pilots will also learn that nerves make for botched up landings. My first attempt was more crash than landing. My check instructor took over the controls from me and gave me an earful. His words have lasted me a lifetime.

'Tell yourself to relax', he said. He didn't ask me to relax. He told me to tell myself to do it. Remarkably, in everything he said, he was training me, like any Guru, to be on my own.

I managed to relax and showed three good landings after that first miss. I wasn't sure if I had qualified yet. The instructor asked the ground crew to refuel the aircraft and turned to me.

'Are you confident?', he asked.

I smiled and nodded.

'Sure?' He asked again... and after a pause which seemed like eternity, he said 'Don't break the bird'. These words still ring in my ears like music after so many years... and I still get goose bumps thinking of the moment. He then proceeded to brief me.

I was to take off and do two circling approaches and execute a 'full stop' landing of the third one. In the first two, I was to abandon my approach from 100 feet above ground.

Woohoo! I was so close now, I thought. And just as I was bracing myself to take on the bird all by myself, someone came running to me and asked me to return to the crew room. The winds had changed to easterly, so we would have to change runway and the weather was looking not too conducive either. I'd have to wait for the following day. What's more, I'd have to repeat the check sortie with the instructor!

To my relief, the skies had cleared the next morning and after a quick briefing, we had completed the sortie and it was time to go solo. I was more confident and mentally prepared now. My instructor accompanied me to the aircraft and watched from above the glass canopy to see if I was doing the start-up procedures right.

As I taxied out with the seat next to me empty the first time, the reality of the moment sank in. I was responsible for this machine now, there was no one to tell me what was going wrong or to take over the controls if it did. I patted the empty seat next to mine and hummed a tune – just the way my instructor did. Doing my checks as I was taught, I was now lined up for takeoff.

As I opened full power and the engine came to life, I thought I felt my mum and dad smiling with me. Even

God, that elusive one, seemed to come a little closer, to look upon me more kindly in that moment. Takeoff was a piece of cake and I was up and away! What a feeling to be all alone in the air! It was nothing like I had imagined it would be. It was more exhilarating and enthralling than anything I could have imagined. I was completely overawed by it all. The humming continued... *'Aa chal ke tujhe mai le ke chalu... ek aise gagan ke tale... jahan gam bhi na ho...'* it went something like that. It was as if I was singing to the airplane who was my darling now. My instructor also used to hum a tune when he was happy and the sortie going smooth. So why shouldn't I? *'Uthe sabke kadam... tara rum-pum-pum....'*

I came in for the first approach and since I didn't have to land this time, I just aimed the aircraft down towards the runway and went around for another circuit.

My instructor called up on the radio and said that I could land at the next approach if I was comfortable. I went about the approach confidently but as I came in to land, I felt that I was too fast and coming in too steep. My speed was building up when it shouldn't have in landing configuration. I wondered what was wrong. Since I wasn't in full control of the situation, I decided to open power and go around for another approach. The song was quite forgotten now and a little panic was creeping in. Would

I be able to land the plane safely? Would I be the first in my batch to fail my first solo flight? Would my parents be smiling still? What would the instructor have to say? What will I say to my friends in the evening? Was it some silly mistake that would make me a laughing stock of the Academy? What about the damage to the expensive machine? Would I be hurt? What if I was to be injured and unable to fly again? All these thoughts flashed across my mind but my training had taught me to not let my mind waver and focus on the problem at hand.

What had gone wrong? What had I forgotten? I went over the procedures in my head and ran my eyes over the controls and dials around me. Then, I noticed the flap meter. On downwind one is supposed to put down a lever to adjust the flaps for landing, or what we used to call 'flaps to takeoff' at the time. In the process of aligning to the runway, one had to put down the lever another notch to 'full flaps'. This helped reduce the speed for landing. I had forgotten to put down the lever the first time, so when I did so on approach to the runway and after aligning for landing, the setting was still on 'flaps to takeoff'. No wonder the craft wasn't slowing down enough for landing.

There was silence in the cockpit. Enough tomfoolery, I remember saying to myself. I concentrated and did every little thing as I had been formally taught to, as if my instructor was sitting beside me. The aircraft did what we call a 'kisser' of a landing and as soon as I cleared the runway, my instructor's voice came up on the radio. He had positioned himself at the edge of the runway, close to the landing point for his pupil's first solo. If the kissing squeal of the tires had been music to my ears, the instructors voice crackling over the radio saying, 'Good landing Saate!' (in his typical easterner accent) was the spring in my feet.

I jumped down the ladder, kissed the machine in respect and started my walk to the crew room, helmet in hand, elated and thoughtful all at once. Closer to the crew room, I heard clapping and cheering. I can never forget the image of a gang of friends, all fellow cadets in blue overalls, waving out to me in congratulations. All of them had gathered near the ATC tower to see the first of our batch complete his first solo sortie. The crew too welcomed me back on terra-firma with smiles and applause. As per tradition, I would send them a box of sweets in gratitude for their support a little later.

That day, I suspect I grew a few inches taller and so I will be for as long as I get to fly on the wings of a bird.

Happy Landings, Empee

Reheat.

Afterburners on.

Rolling for takeoff.

In the wee hours of the morning of 20 May 2014, my friend and course mate, 'Empee' got on his way into the blue skies. Having been literally tied down to a wheel chair for a half of his life, he was finally free – to do as he liked, to do what he liked best, to fly high in the sky.

When he took off for his final flight, Empee had spent 50 years and 15 days on this planet. The writing was on the wall, we had been told by the doctors just short of his 50th birthday. He had the deadly blood cancer and there was no way out. But more deadly than the disease that claimed his life was the accident that made him a quadriplegic.

In early 1988, Empee had graduated at the top of his class as a fighter pilot. He had taken to the cockpit like a natural. But he was as studious as he was instinctive. He spent a lot of time preparing for his sorties and analysing his performance thereafter. He was also known for reading voraciously. His wide knowledge in the field of aviation made him a sort of 'Gen-master' of his squadron. Friends and seniors sought his help if they were to understand some intricate aspects of aerodynamics or the latest in navigation systems.

On 28th of June 1988, Flying Officer MP Anil Kumar, a strapping, promising young fighter pilot met with a freak motorcycle accident in Pathankot, an accident that transformed his life forever and took him from being 'airborne' to a 'chair borne' warrior. For 26 years, Empee was paralysed neck down and confined to a wheelchair. But a warrior he remained nevertheless. Incidentally, 'Airborne to Chair-borne' was the title of his personal account of how he fought life and his quadriplegia, a memoir that launched him into the field of serious writing.

Now that Empee is gone, all there is to do is cherish the memories he left behind – Empee in a colourful *lungi* and a matching shirt, up and about early. Empee having breakfast in bed with his favourite *mallu* songs or glued to the news on TV. Empee being wheeled to his computer by the window, painstakingly researching and writing his articles. Right across the fields from Empee's window in the Kirkee Paraplegic Home were fighters getting airborne at the Air Force base while visitors wait to meet Empee. They see him first through this window, he nods his head and the pencil in his mouth drops into his lap. The wheelchair is brought out in the corridor and a few chairs for the visitors. Empee insists on a particular placement of his chair so that he can keep an eye on the sky for the fighters.

Some visitors are ill at ease to meet him for the first time but the warmth and confidence he exudes melts away all the inhibitions. Empee has a way of putting everyone at ease with his wit and humour. He has a variety of visitors – fellow paraplegics to batch-mates to young students of school and colleges, not to forget his 'school-types' from Sainik School, Kazhakootam. He gets along like wild fire with all of them, expressing his views on any topic thrown at him. Once you know him, you want to hold on to him, return to meet him again and again, such is his magnetic charm.

I visit Empee in Kirkee every time I am on annual leave in Pune. One day, I find him in a frenzy, feverishly tracking his correspondence with the Indian Air Force and the Government of India. A cadet involved in an air accident in the final stage of his training and paralysed waist down, is to be boarded out and sent home with no benefits as per the policy in vogue. But Empee is not one to back down. He fights the established norms and demands a humane view for the plight of the cadet. Finally, the cadet is granted commission as an officer on a wheelchair. Empee's victory is the first such case in the history of the Armed Forces in India. Empee makes us so proud.

His discipline, his perfection and his dogged determination in fighting for what is rightfully due make him a loved, yet feared inmate at the paraplegic home. All inmates turn to him to resolve their problems and issues and he is the *de-facto* leader of the home. Through his constant engagements with the management, he ensures that the good quality of life promised to the inmates is delivered in practice.

Empee is a stickler for perfection and his demands for order in the smallest things – such as his cupboard – makes us pull our hair sometimes! One day, Empee wants me to read one of the articles that he has written. I am made to go to the place and given perfect instructions – 'look in the left pile of magazines near the window, the third one from the top, page 72 to 74. And after you read it please keep it back in the same place.'

So well researched and grammatically correct are the

articles he sends his publishers, that editors have nothing to do but upload them on the website. Empee also makes it a point to remember little details that mean something to you. He can remember the date, day and time that he met you, what you were wearing, what the weather was like on the day, he remembers your birthday and anniversary, the names of your children. I, like many of his friends, treasure the signed-by-mouth cards that I received on my birthday without fail, every year.

It is 2014. In a special corner of the ICU reserved for him, Empee is celebrating his 50th birthday in style. He has decided the guest list, presided over the preparations, given explicit instructions to everyone as to how his day is to be celebrated. He has finalised the menu – cup cakes from Monginis, *samosa*s from his favourite shop in Kirkee market, no non-veg items and tea/coffee. He has made a guest list, calculated the costs and reconciled them with his budget, all from the ICU. Someone suggests he invite a certain senior officer. 'If we call him he will come with his entire entourage and that will be the end of my party!' quips Empee, ever witty as well as practical. This is the last time that we are to see him as we have known him – sharp, alive and kicking.

A little later, we, his friends are to see him slip in and out of coma. Sometimes, he opens his eyes and we find in them, the same recognition, the wit and the humour as if he is picking up on a conversation from where he left off. When he is coherent, he argues with the doctor that he should be at his computer as soon as possible.

'You see all this running around for chemo has resulted in a whole lot of correspondence piling up on my computer', he says and we wonder if he has grasped the nearness of death. 'I can come at the time that you ask me to and can go back to my room immediately after that...', he continues. Then, as we fear his loosening grip on reality, he adds without skipping a beat. 'I would like to die in my own bed. I hope you know that.'

Empee's pet line comes to mind when Empee breaks his earthly shackles. 'The greater the difficulty, the sweeter the victory.' He was born to be free, the Almighty put him to a hard test and here too he passed with flying colours. Happy landings, Empee!

PS. In 2016, I wrote the biopic on the life of Flying Officer MP Anil Kumar titled, *Born to Fly*.

The helicopter is probably the most versatile instrument ever invented by man. It approaches closer than any other to fulfillment of mankind's ancient dreams of the flying horse and the magic carpet.

—Igor Sikorsky

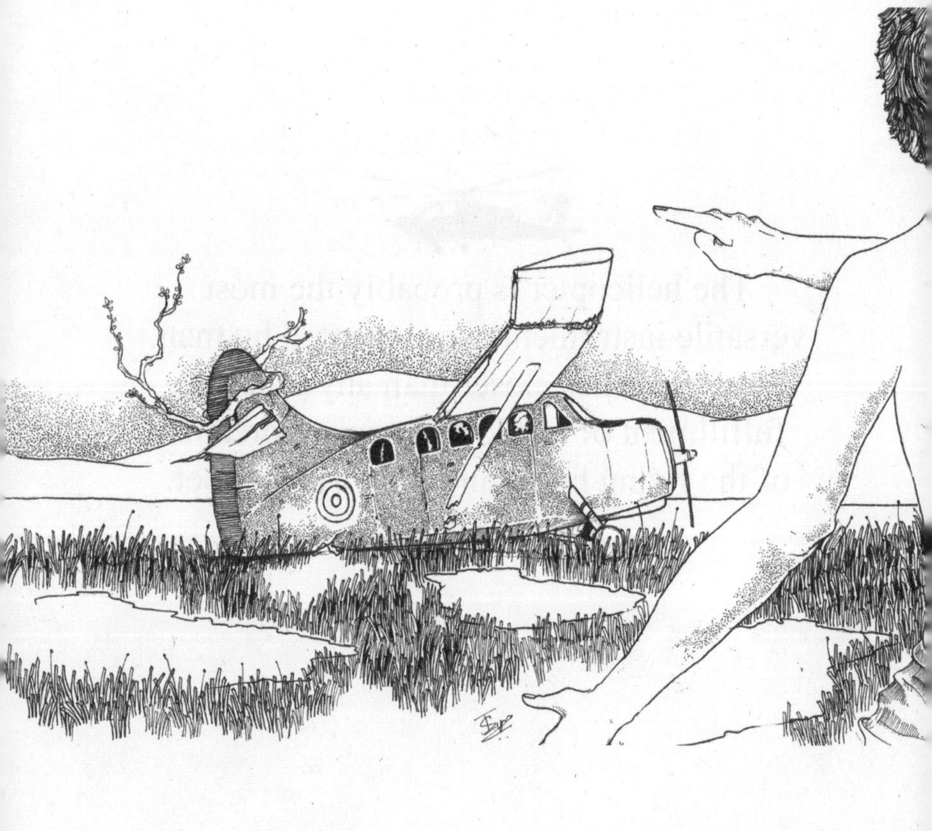

Have Wings, Will Fly

An Otter had to be lifted by helicopter and brought back to base for repairs. The year was 1989 and these small aircraft, de Havilland Otters, were soon going to be confined to the museums. One of the few machines flying was on a routine sortie from Guwahati to Hashimara and had an emergency which warranted a force landing in a field close to the river Brahmaputra. The young pilot, Flying Officer Sanjay Gupta or Goofy as he was called, took actions as per his emergency checklist and saved the aircraft and its occupants from certain death. Here is how it happened in Goofy's own words:

'We had around 7-8 passengers on board and it was a single pilot operation. The weather was clear skies and I started on

time for Hashi. Somewhere over Kokrajhar district, the engine coughed a couple of times and all of sudden, the whole aircraft shuddered quite violently and the engine stopped. I was flying at an altitude of 4,500 feet, had just crossed a small range of slightly hilly terrain and I could see paddy fields around with mighty river Brahmaputra to my left. I immediately put the aircraft into a glide, turned right and instinctively selected an area for a Forced Landing. At the back of my mind, I was aware that this was a disturbed area, ours was an IAF aircraft and definitely a target. But an aircraft with no thrust gives you no options. And, the Otter aircraft had poor glide capabilities. I had time only for one MAYDAY call, looked back over my shoulders to shout a warning to the passengers to sit tight and started pumping the flaps down as I commenced a left turn to align the aircraft with the selected field for landing. This was almost parallel to a road. As the field was full of water, I decided to make it a 3-pointer landing, as slow as possible. This was to avoid toppling over.

It was a beautiful landing, I must say. It was all over in less than 5 minutes, from sitting alone in the cockpit, with my side window down and open, enjoying the weather and the view to sitting on ground and trying to catch attention of any aircraft with a MAYDAY call. An Alliance Do-228 picked it up and relayed same to Guwahati ATC. I think the passengers were in a bit of a shock. I called one Lt Col and requested him to go out, catch the first available transport and approach police. I had another IAF officer and few airmen on board. I asked him to make a small team and surround the aircraft to prevent people from approaching the aircraft. And, I climbed up on to the aircraft, sat on the wing and waited for the relief helicopter.'

After the pilot and the passengers were taken to safety, it was time to retrieve the machine for what it was worth.

The crew was carefully chosen. The stakes were high because it had to be lifted over populated areas and a small error, even misjudgement, could spell disaster. We were asked to practise for the mission at the airbase close to the runway. An aeroplane without an engine was chosen from the hangar as the practice dummy. As such, the old bird had lived its life. Some sandbags were placed inside the cabin to simulate the actual weight of the machine that lay in the fields. It was dragged into the sun in between the runway and the taxi track and shackled for the lift. The detailed brief to the crew included what would happen if the load 'misbehaved' in flight. On the day fixed for the simulated retrieval, a large number of spectators – families of officers and men – from the airbase gathered to watch the operation. Some passengers travelling out of the Guwahati airport at that hour were also lucky to view the spectacle! Whirling its rotors at max rpm, our helicopter got airborne for a dummy circuit to ensure that we followed a path without or with minimum habitation below. Then we came to a steady hover over the Otter. The airframe quivered, dust and debris flew upwards. Not much could be heard above the din of the rotors. On the ground, the crew appeared in their protective gear and got the shackles attached to the underbelly of the helicopter and gave thumbs up. We took the helicopter vertically upwards to take off the slack in the cable and lift the aeroplane clear of the ground before it began its forward flight. All seemed to be well.

The crowd must have looked on in admiration as one aeroplane lifted another. As the helicopter picked up speed and gained height, the plane below began to swing a bit. And then, in a blink of an eye, it started flying back to mother earth. For some reason, the shackle had come loose. In a matter of seconds, the pilotless and engineless plane did a jig in the sky and crashed near the runway. A cloud of dust arose from the wet and soggy ground when the sandbags burst open upon impact. It was broken in so many places that it was only fit for the junkyard now. A rescue party rushed to the site to check if anyone was injured and to take precautions against the wreckage catching fire. The exercise was shelved. The helicopter crew returned, disappointed and shaken.

In order to find out the cause of the accident, a court of inquiry (CoI) was ordered. This is mandatory in all cases of unusual occurrence, especially when there is loss of life or property. A senior helicopter pilot from an adjoining base was assigned to this CoI, along with a team of two – one technical expert and one pilot to help in the investigations. As per procedure, all aspects and facts leading to the accident were looked at. Whether the crew had had adequate rest, whether they had had breakfast on that particular day, whether they were medically fit and seen by the doctor during the briefing, whether they were adequately briefed, whether the technicians had done their jobs meticulously, whether there was some evidence to suggest sabotage – the simplest and the most absurd theories were considered. All people involved were questioned as in a typical court room and their answers recorded, signed and authenticated.

While the court did its job, crew rooms, both in the helicopter and the Otter squadrons were abuzz with discussions and theories of what could have happened. The conversations in the evenings at the bar would also invariably veer towards what had happened, how it could have transpired. As the evening progressed, the theories became more enthusiastic and less logical of course.

Some people floated the theory that one of the crew had accidentally pressed the emergency release switch. Another group wanted to blame the technicians for not ensuring that the equipment was serviceable. Someone also called it an act of God and asked for a *havan* to be conducted to ward off evil spirits and thank the Almighty to have saved the people on the ground. So much discussion was bound to lead to fiery agreements and disagreements, while tempers flared between the units and things were not as happy as they generally are.

The crew of the helicopter went through a harrowing time repeating their story to all and sundry. But no one could give a plausible reason why such a thing could have happened. So they all waited for the enquiry to come out with the answer. Most people became convinced that the case would remain unresolved for want of evidence.

The court of inquiry did resolve the matter. It came up with the simplest of explanations: As the helicopter gained speed, the 'rescued' airplane with its wings hanging below also decided to fly i.e. its wings produced a lift with wind blowing over them. So the aircraft by itself, gained height and the attachment to the underbelly of the helicopter loosened. The automatic release mechanism in the helicopter understood this as a signal that the aircraft being lifted had touched the ground and so the cable was released.

The court recommended that in future, if such an exercise was to be undertaken, the wings of the aeroplane needed to be removed and transported rather than be fixed to the fuselage. As far as the poor aircraft which had landed in the fields was concerned, no one wanted to take the risk of lifting it by helicopter now. The orders were passed to have it broken down into manageable parts and moved back to base by trucks.

So simple and no one thought of it until then. Although there were a few guys who went around with that look that said 'I knew it all along but no one was listening to me'!

In the Wake of the Giant

Eight years after I left the island and nine years after the tsunami of 2004, I return to the Car Nicobar air base for a short visit. I have wanted very much to see for myself the resurgence of the islands in the years following the catastrophe and subsequent rebuilding, of which I was fortunate to be a part.

I am both happy and sad at what I see. New homes stand on stilts, local businesses seem to be thriving, shops are flush with items, the roads are busy with honking traffic and the markets are full with shoppers. The touch of the tsunami is still evident however. The small lakes formed as a result of the sudden onslaught of the sea exist as marshes. In the pieces of concrete sticking out of the sand, in the broken, coloured corals lying around on the beaches, in the sunken ship out in the waters, in the broken houses in ghost villages darkened by dust and moisture, the devastation of the tsunami remains in view. In some ways, the island is fresh and new. Yet, it will never be the same again.

I attend a lovely social evening at the 'new' officers' mess at the air base and find everyone eager to hear my experiences as a member of the rescue and rehabilitation mission. As I relate those stories, my mind is like a film reel going backwards. Even as I get into bed for the night, my mind continues to replay the old days, the people and conversations that I had not thought about in a long time.

'Baba, do you know what a *soo*nami is?' asks my 9-year old.

She is tugging at my sleeve as I stoke a fire outside my shack of a home in Patiala. At the turn of 2004-05, friends and family have gathered at my place for drinks and dinner.

'*Baba*! What is a *soo*nami?' she asks again.

I haven't the faintest idea. My daughter drags me to the bedroom TV where news channels are describing a tragedy that has struck that morning. They're making much of the destruction caused by a large wave that rose out of the sea unannounced. How large can a large wave be after all? Thanks to my lack of information at the time, I dismiss it to be a minor disaster that will soon be forgotten like the disasters that are reported in the news every day. I return to conversations in front of the fire. More news filters in as the night carries on and the gigantic proportions of the tragedy begin to become clear to those of us on the mainland. I wonder about how my friends in Car Nicobar are doing. I imagine they are contributing to the relief and rescue operations as always. But when I call up my friends in Air HQ, I find that they are as much victims of the tragedy as rescuers of victims. Only counting AF personnel and families, we have lost over 120 lives. The AF station is in ruins as most of the buildings have been razed to the ground. The entire island of 10 km by 12 km has been hit from all sides – the total death toll is expected to be in the hundreds, maybe in the thousands. There is no news from many of the smaller islands to the south. With the scale of natural destruction, the remote islands could even have been entirely consumed by the sea.

My immediate reaction is to volunteer on one of the rescue missions. I tell my boss in Delhi who tries to talk me out of my enthusiasm. Something tells me to raise the ante. I call up more people in Delhi. To my relief, my name has already been proposed to be sent for the mission and approved by the Chief of Air Staff himself. I am to leave a very worried family behind as I leave for the mission to Car Nic.

We take off on a rattling AN-32. On the long flight, I

observe the men and officers who are going to be part of the team. While some have determined looks on their faces, others look worried. They all have been 'detailed' for the adventure. I reckon it is easier for me because I volunteered for this. However, past experience in the AF tells me that with a little motivation and a few days on the island, these men will be as good as anyone who volunteered. We are seven officers in charge of 70 men. Besides our own frugal belongings, we have radio sets, some medicines, emergency rations, some basic tools like shovels and axes and some water which will last for a day at most.

We finally land on the island after 4 hours of flying over the vast expanse of the Bay of Bengal and as we descend to land, we get our first glimpse of the shattered island. The mention of beaches always makes one think of sandy stretches with serene waters. This is far from it. The sea is still angry. We see a large number of trees, parts of the homes, cars and other debris floating aimlessly in the churning brown waters. The radar ramp is broken on both sides with the antenna vehicle hanging precariously from the edge. Smoke is rising from one corner of the airfield. The runway at one end seems to have disappeared under water and survivors dot the edges of what remains of it. Large, 80,000 litre diesel tanks belonging to Indian Oil lie toppled over on their sides blocking the entry into the AF station area.

The aircraft taxies through water. As soon as the doors are open, we are greeted by the smell of the sea along with the smell of rotting flora and fauna. The stench overpowers us and lodges itself deep in our brains. It won't bother us so much in a few days. We will get used to it but even after we leave the island, we will never forget it. Our friends are waiting for us on the tarmac. Many have lost their near and dear ones. They cannot speak of the hell that they have lived through. Some are distraught. Others smile stoically in welcome. Barring a few of the old lot who will stay with us for two more days to 'hand over' what is left of the airbase, the rest are going back immediately.

There is no time to lose. We split into our areas of responsibility and try to understand the Hows and the Whys of things. Oblivious of time, we try to do what needs to be done and along the way we hear individual escapades of the survivors. Death is everywhere. It has touched everyone we meet on the island. Despite the chaos, we need to make sure the men on the rehab team are reasonably well settled and well rested. The tents are erected in an orderly manner which restores some semblance of order to our living area at least. Eventually, cook houses, bath areas, water storage, ration storage, medical room, ops rooms – all that is required for everyday life of an air station will be set up in these tents in some form or other. In a few weeks, we will even have a small volleyball court made with a net strung over a cleared area of land.

We spend our first evening over a frugal meal getting to know each other better and planning for the next day. The next morning, we are up and about before the sun has risen over the sea. There is a lot to be done. An aircraft will soon arrive to pick up the final lot of survivors. We go to see them off and wish them well. The AF personnel who served on the islands and braved the tsunami hold a wealth of experience. We try and get as much information from them before the aircraft takes off with them. When they leave, we are like shipwrecked sailors marooned on an island in the middle of the ocean. We are so far away from what we know to be 'real' life. Our adventure on the island has only just begun.

The first thing for us to do is to get the debris sorted out. We decide to begin with the runway first. We need to make it operational for more aeroplanes to fly in with food and material from the mainland. But nothing is simple after nature has run over it in its fury. The runway needs major repairs for which we will require about 80 tons of a quick drying resin compound. We will also require specialist equipment which will be three times the weight of this raw material. We cannot stall movement of aircraft so there is no way we can repair the runway at one go. Temporary repairs will have to be made after each take off and landing. This will take up a lot of manpower during which time other tasks will suffer.

After a few days of trial and error and all kinds of planning going awry, we realise we must put in place a decision matrix and some rules of logic to be able to manage a little of this and a little of that and make sure we are moving in an overall constructive and positive direction. Everyone is in a hurry to get his area of responsibility in order. There is pulling and tugging for man and material within the sub-teams. Sometimes, there is political pressure to get relief to a particular island or send more material to another. Above all this, the steady stream of 'VIP' visitors coming for what we call 'disaster tourism' doesn't cease. In this situation, the only way one can plan is to be ready to change the plan. After all, an effective plan is only one that can deliver tangible results. In this 'take-it-as-it-comes' high-stakes disaster situation, there are lessons in team psychology, disaster management and project planning for everyone on the rescue and rehab team.

In our first week on the island, we are inundated with stories of survival and rescue. A girl who floated on a piece of broken door in the ocean has been rescued alive after two days. Unfortunately, all her family has perished. A boy stuck atop a coconut tree for three days is found to have survived on a bottle of Sprite, which miraculously got stuck in the tree along with him. A pregnant lady has been rescued from the third storey of a house as the lower storeys were being washed away from under her.

One of the most telling tales concerns the locals and the district administration. Apparently the local fishermen had noticed a certain red coloured fish in their nets a few days before the earthquake that caused the tsunami. Local, handed-down wisdom told them that red fish, which lives near the ocean floor, only comes up to the surface when it senses vibrations under the earth. The local community had warned the administration but their concerns had been dismissed as being influenced by folklore. For all the tsunami warning systems that were set up around the world after the tsunami, there were already some warning systems that we hadn't utilised! How many lives may have been saved if modern science had simply been in touch with traditional science? How much destruction can still be averted in the world if man listens, really listens to his fellow man!

We have all been trained to stay in tents and camp in the open and survive off the land during our training. But training always leaves room for learning and adapting in real life situations. This is like training but it is real! We have to set up a quasi-permanent home in the tents. There are three to four of us to one; no privacy, just community living. Water is placed just outside the tents in drums. Once in a while, the cows and other domestic animals come in, desperate for water and pull away at the ropes holding the tents in place. There are snakes, cerebral malaria-causing mosquitoes and other reptiles to deal with too. One has to be careful when one goes into the open for the morning do.

Living away from their families takes a toll on the men. To be surrounded by destruction and to find the will to rebuild from scratch extracts an emotional price as well as a physical one. While some of us do all we can to maintain the morale of our teams in this situation, someone starts off a rumour that the island is so damaged that it will sink into the ocean any day, letting none of us escape alive. The gullible in our teams go into a panic. I have a large number of applications on my desk the next morning asking for withdrawal from the area for safety reasons. When the rumour monger is taken to task and unceremoniously put on a flight back to the mainland, some order and faith is restored.

One has to cajole the men, speak to them often to remind them and impress upon them the significance of our work here. One has always to keep them busy – be it work or play. We stick together even after working hours. There is really nowhere else to go. We sing and pray and play together. We try to have as much rest as possible. Yet, motivation remains an issue. I have a laptop like satellite phone which is to be used only for official purposes. After trying many ways of lifting the morale of the teams, we find that if we allow the phone to be used by each one for a short call home once every week, everyone's official productivity leaps! This is a classic example to show that when the leadership begins to understand the people in their teams, not as earmarked resources but as humans not much different from themselves, they can find the simplest, most effective ways of boosting morale and productivity.

Working alongside different agencies, all involved in relief work but all with different short-term approaches, priorities and political affiliations is tricky. Sometimes, it is also amusing! There is this instance when a man from the local administration wants to send a100 kits of relief with a hundred litres of milk to an island which has a total population of 17 people! No amount of reasoning works with him since he is being ordered to do so by his higher ups. So we load up the 100 kits and send them to another island where they can be utilised!

Work on the island is relentless. Men are eating between offloading/loading one aeroplane and clearing the tarmac for the next one. Some are eating while filing the day's reports and some while showing around a senior official on a visit. There is always something immediate to attend to. I have trained in the National Defence Academy and I know what it is to be tired. But the days of being a cadet had only physical exhaustion. This tiredness is one of responsibility and expectation, of working towards a goal that has to be met at any cost. The last thing I remember thinking of before sleep takes over is the sound of the sea and my to-do list for the next day.

I am woken by a tremble. The ground is shaking and a tsunami warning is sounding in the distance. I sit up in bed. I am not in a tent anymore. I am in the new officers' mess in the new airbase on which we had begun work over eight years ago. This is the very area that lay strewn with debris when we had seen it from the An-32 on our first flight into the island. I smile to myself. The tsunami warning is fading off. The earth is quiet again. So many years after the tsunami, on the one evening that I return to the island, it is as if Mother Nature has orchestrated a shake-up only for me! Maybe she means to remind me that I may have been part of a historic rebuilding but that nature's work and ours remains ever unfinished.

PS. A year later, I was able to pen down my experiences of the tsunami and the aftermath in my first book titled, *A Few Good Men & the Angry Sea*.

Just for a Fag

In the times of civil unrest and mass violence in Congo, the premises of the UN troops were arguably the most secure place that one could be in. I was part of the UN forces in Goma, Congo. Our camp was located close to the town. One pocket was near the hangers and the airfield and a second, where we lived, was about a kilometre away. There was a wide rift in the Congolese army and news of brutality was commonplace. We were all doing our best to cool things down and naturally, for this 'intervention', we were constantly under threat.

The entire camp had double layered fencing around it with watch towers to provide for good visibility and mutual support. Within it, we lived in portable cabins that were well-ventilated and air-conditioned and we had that rare luxury in the African continent – 24 hours of uninterrupted power supply. In the heart of darkness, we were as comfortable as we could possibly be. The contingents of different countries lived in camps alongside each other and guards from each of these were tasked with patrolling the fence at all times of the day and night.

Goma can get quite cold at night and fog habitually descends forming a thick cover by midnight. These are not welcome conditions for the men doing guard duty. It was some consolation that some of our men were used to lower temperatures and more hardships guarding our Indian borders and the good fellows never complained. I had a young airman colleague on duty on this night I speak of. He was a young lad, barely a few years into military life. From the neighbouring camps, sounds of music and merriment fell on his ears ever so often on the lonely nights he spent patrolling the fence, trying to stay alert to the first signs of intrusion. I wouldn't blame him if he longed for a night of partying and revelry too, every once in a while.

A few months prior to this night, one of the guards had been caught misbehaving with a local woman. This sort of incident is intolerable anywhere but it is uglier still when it happens in a foreign land where anything a soldier does is taken to be a representation of his country. The offending guard in this case had been sent home pronto. Everybody on the Indian contingent had been duly warned by the security officer. We hoped that the threat of instant and dishonourable deportation to the homeland would be deterrent enough. There's no doubt that the dollars that one gave up on, if sent home early, was an equal threat.

On this foggy night in Goma, as one of our airmen guarded the boundary of the camp, his rifle pointed downwards, he heard a rustle in the shrubs outside the gate. Carefully, ready for action, when he went out to investigate, he was met with a sight I doubt he will ever forget. In the glare of his flashlight, three men were standing in nothing but their underwear, their eyes glazed, no coherent words escaping their lips. It would have been comic if it wasn't for the war-ravaged conditions that surrounded us. Were they booby trapped? Was this a terrorist attack? What could they hide in their underwear? The guard radioed for help.

There was commotion in the camp as an alarm was raised and almost everyone was out of their 'porta-cabins' and on their guard. When help arrived for the lone guard faced with an unlikely trio, to our relief and surprise, the three men were found to be drunk, probably drugged but not terrorists for sure. On being identified as being on the UN contingent, they were wrapped into blankets and left to sleep for the night. A roll call later, it was confirmed that no one was missing from our camp.

The next morning, before they faced the dire consequences that awaited them, the other chaps made sure to wrangle the story out of the trio. From what we were able to piece together, this is what happened.

A simple way of keeping the gusto of troops going, especially in trying operational situations is to provide them the small luxury of evening parties as often as possible. Fortunately, UN contingents are rather well looked after when it comes to food and drink and there was a party in one or the other camp almost every night. That night, there had been a party inside a hangar located near the airfield. The poor guards on patrolling duty were possibly the only ones left behind. The party had wound up early and most men had returned to their respective camps. The men in-charge of organising, the now infamous trio, were the last ones to leave since they had to wind up for the night. After the trucks had been loaded with unused stocks, they are said to have decided to smoke one last cigarette before they returned. None had any cigarettes left however. So, tired as they were, they did not back out and simply go home. On their way back to their camp, they took a detour to a nearby pub. They were intent on having their last fag of the night.

At one time, Goma used to be famous for its nightlife

but the civil war had given that reputation a beating. Even so, the pub that the men entered was flashy and inviting, replete with women bartenders, offering drinks and winking at curious bystanders in invitation. Already inebriated from their party and smitten by a particular busty bartender, the three men decided to take a table and have a few beers. Before they knew it, there were three beautiful women in the place of one. They were swinging beer bottles in their hands and smiling mischievously. The three men could not have hoped for a better finale to their party. They probably already imagined how they would boast of it to the other fellows the next day.

The invitation to stay for 'just one more beer' must have been accepted many times over because it was many beers and many dances later that the men got up to pay for their drinks and cigarettes and leave. Even when making the most inane mistakes, a small voice in a soldier's head always cries in the voice of a senior. There was much to answer for if one got back to camp later than permitted. To stay out so late into the night, the men should have gotten out-passes before they left. Security regulations and soldierly discipline meant that they were really not allowed instinctive stopovers at bars at odd hours. Sometimes, the forbidding voice of a senior only cries out when it is too late.

Now there is nothing surprising about the way this story ends. What do you expect? Just as they rose to leave, the men were robbed of everything but their underwear and beaten by a crowd of energetic, drunken Congolese more than willing to vent their angst on unknown foreigners. Of course, by the time they escaped in the direction of their camp, the drugs that they had been administered through the beer had begun to take effect. Small mercies then, that they had no recollection of the catcalls from the jeering late-nighters in the streets of Goma. Besides a hurt ego and a dent in their wallets, they were thankful to be alive, even if not so thankful about having to tell the tale.

I am amazed at how smart young men, trained to keep their heads in far more dangerous situations will fall for a known bait over and over again. Young men never seem to learn from the history of other young men who have gone before them.

All this: just for a fag?

The helicopter is a fine way to travel, but it induces a view of the world that only God and CEOs sharc on a rcgular basis.

—Morley Safer

Nyiragongo

I was on top of the world. Or so I thought. Everything but the pale blue sky seemed to me to be laid out before me from where I stood peering down the lip of the volcano. I was literally looking into a hole in the mountain. In it, a lake of molten lava swelled and smouldered, an intense, kinetic painting in orange and black. Occasionally, the mountain rumbled beneath our feet, as if a resident giant was turning on his side and grunting from the effort. Sulphurous smoke filled my nostrils. I heard others in my group coughing away the irritation caused by the fumes. We were atop the famed Nyiragongo volcano, one of the few live volcanoes in the world.

At the summit, everyone from our enthusiastic bunch

turned silent, as if stunned by the sheer energy of the volcano. The most extravagant sights in nature make one turn inward. Standing there, I felt small and insignificant, incredulous, yet happy. As much as we crave attention and importance in our everyday lives, a reminder of the relative magnitude of things is unfailingly liberating.

The mouth of the Nyiragongo volcano is about 4,000 feet or 1.2 kilometres wide. Every time we saw it from the air, it beckoned to us and one wished one could fly right down into its mouth! Even though I had seen it from air, nothing could have prepared me for the size of the volcano when standing on it. I wondered about what would happen if I fell in. I imagined a man would be consumed in seconds and be gone without a trace. Remarkably, the thought didn't invoke fear. Usually, one fears even an overheated oven or boiling water if one begins to think of how it could cause bodily harm. But standing at the lip of that gigantic pool of fire and earth that was boiling at 1,200 degrees Centigrade, I felt only expanse and lightness, almost an attraction to the bottomless mysteries of the volcano.

Volcanic ash was being constantly swept up by the wind. I looked back at the rest of my group. Like large snowflakes of grey, the ash dangled from their hair and got stuck to their eyebrows. I smiled to myself. It made us all look like actors with bad makeup from the Hindi movies of old.

When we had arrived in the Democratic Republic of Congo (DRC) as part of the UN peace keeping mission, this smoky mountain had been our symbol of getaway. We could see it from our camp as from anywhere in the open country around it. Doing *surya namaskar* in the morning atop a *machan* in the camp was like offering prayers to this natural wonder. When we flew in the area, the smoke could be seen from miles during the day and the orange glow lit up the sky at night. In fact, the volcano served as one of the reporting points for pilots when coming in to land at the airfield in Goma.

The volcano had had a major eruption only three years before we set foot on it. Molten lava had flowed down the mountain causing widespread destruction, markers of which were present everywhere. Locals told us that the lava flow had stopped just a few meters from the shores of the giant lake, Kivu. This lake is known to have vast reserves of methane gas under its surface, which if ignited by the lava could have caused a tsunami like wave spelling doom for the busy and beautiful town of Goma at the edge of the lake. The locals had prayed to the volcano, we were told, and so the disaster had been averted. The town of Goma had been sliced into two parts by the lava and when seen from the air, a black line could still be seen where the lava had once flown. The runway itself had been cut into two parts. Stranded jetliners from that time had become relics of the airfield. The locals had stripped these aeroplanes of whatever they could make use of. Local children loitering across the airfield now used the vestigial airframes to hide and play in.

Nyiragongo was on the list of recommended 'Must-Dos' handed down to us by the previous contingent to the UN. Kilimanjaro in Tanzania was another inviting proposition on the list but it would have taken up all of our week-long authorised leave and much more planning besides. So it happened that in a group of four, we decided to tackle Nyiragongo first. Having erupted more than 35 times in recorded history, the Nyiragongo volcano is described as being the most dangerous in the world. We had seen a minor eruption during one of our night flying sorties a few months prior to our trip. After that experience, the thought of scaling the volcano had become even more exciting to us.

We had to prepare to be self sufficient for 36 odd hours and that required intricate planning. Right from the smallest things like extra pairs of laces to a first aid kit for all kinds of common emergencies and injuries, torches, small knives, insect repellents – we made multiple lists of must-haves and good-to-haves because every kilo of weight on our backs would add to the difficulty of the climb. We decided on 15 kg as the maximum limit for each person's backpack. We had been told about a small hut that had been built by a Japanese scientific expedition a few years earlier. The hut was only a short way from the summit and it would house us for the night.

A crisp, chilly morning awaited us on the day chosen for the adventure. The chill in the air made our noses water as we set course for the base of the mountain in our jeeps. When we sent back the vehicles from the village at the base of the mountain, some villagers became concerned. A contingent of villagers was sent out to us to enquire why UN troops were attempting to climb the volcano, usually of interest only to the scientific community. The two local guides with us had to pacify them and managed to convince them that these UN troops simply wanted to 'climb for fun'!

We began the ascent. Even for fit and trained military men like us, the climb to the 12,000 feet summit was more challenging than we had imagined. The path was jagged and steep and we were climbing with the assigned 15kgs on our backpacks. The rocky valley did not offer any cushion and a fall was sure to leave one with a grievously memorable injury. In a few hours, our backs hurt from the load and we had to stop numerous times. Even our solid army boots were tested to their limits. Despite their thick soles, sharp rocks managed to poke into our feet. As we gained height, the greenery gave way to more jagged rocks. We were getting dehydrated rapidly and water had to be consumed but rationed as well. We had been warned that there was no source of water on the summit. After over twenty years, I felt like I was reliving the tough regimen of my days in my training academy.

Our porters were two Congolese men who had quit their military jobs for the safer option of becoming porters/guides. Even though they were much older than us, these men easily did the climb with double the size of our backpacks. They did not understand much English and only one of us knew a little French from his French language course at NDA. He became the group's interpreter. So, this was why they had language courses at NDA – the very courses that we had, as cadets, shunned and resisted!

At one of the resting points, one chap from our group realised that a pair of binoculars was missing. At first, he said that he had seen them at the last stop but on being asked repeatedly if he was sure, he began to doubt his memory so much that by the end of the questioning, he had no idea where he may have dropped them. We had climbed for about 45 minutes since the last water break and it was not merely irritating for the rest of us but even a little problematic. The binoculars were a 'controlled item' issued to us for official use. Losing it would entail a formal court of inquiry and certain punishment. Besides the ignominy of the punishment we would have to deal with a brushing down by the seniors. Even if we went back, would we be able to find the place where we had stopped? What if it had fallen right at the beginning of the climb? As we sat discussing our next course of action, one of our porter guides went missing. He seemed to have dropped his load and vanished.

The only thing to do now was to abandon the trip to the summit and set course downwards in search of the errant binoculars. Just as we were getting mentally prepared to retrace our path, the missing man appeared far away on the slopes. He was running towards us shouting what sounded like gibberish, waving out to us with something in his hand. Our man had managed to run down, find the binoculars and come all the way back up in the time that we hadn't been able to come to a decision! He surely won the extra drinks of rum for himself and his mate. These were the guides who we had grudgingly agreed to take along with us because it was part of safety requirements. In the end, they carried much of our additional load – water, coal, food – and brought their experience and knowledge of this land which, as they proved, is often more valuable than the most advanced military training and strategic risk analysis.

A 1,000 odd feet before the summit, we came to the hut where we were to spend the night; only that it had gaping holes in the ceiling and on the sides. So much for protection! But a shelter it was nevertheless and we had no choice either. We piled up our backpacks at the entrance and left our guides there before we attempted the final assault to the summit. The orange glow of the setting sun in the background and the orange glow of the volcano awaited us – one of the most breathtaking sights that I have ever seen.

With the last rays of the sun, we lay down with our backs resting on the lip of the crater, watching the stars as they came into view on a darkening sky. When we got back to our huts, our guides – God bless them! – had cleaned and dusted, laid out our sleeping bags and started a fire inside the hut. To get officer like treatment even at the edge of a volcano. Now who wouldn't like that? Some of us were worried about the smoke killing us in our sleep. Our guides explained to us in French and broken English, or this is what we think they meant to explain. Smoke would not stay inside the hut because hot smoky air, being lighter than the cooler air outside, would rise up to the ceiling and be replaced by cooler air below. The smoky air near the ceiling would be continually sucked away through the holes. We were not entirely convinced but agreed because the hut had so many ventilating holes anyway.

By this time we were a band of ravenous climbers. Without ado, *paratha*s were taken out one by one and held over the fire by another. *Aloo gobi subzi* was served on top of the skewered *paratha*s and served with mango pickle. To wash down the food, we had a tot of rum each before we put our tired limbs into the sleeping bags and chatted ourselves to sleep. But for the rumbling volcano, there was not a sound on the mountain. I remember drifting to sleep watching the light from the volcano and lights of Goma in the distance – on the one hand, the exhilaration of wild, unrestrained nature, on the other, the comforting closeness of civilisation and humankind.

It turned out there was another adventure to contend with before the night was out. Somewhere in the course of the night, I was awakened by something nibbling at my toe. When I turned on the torch, three large rodents stole a look at me and slunk away. I couldn't help shouting out in alarm. This woke the whole group. We spent a few minutes laughing and flashing our torches in all corners of the hut. Finally, we decided to keep a night watchman on rotation duty through the night although I doubt any of us slept soundly after this rodent invasion – none other than our Congolese guides, who reacted to our frenzy only by turning away from the glare of torch light and going back to sleep!

Morning came and marked the beginning of the end of our adventure. A quick breakfast before departure consisted of bread and boiled eggs and to top it all, the luxury of a hot cup of tea which our guides had managed to make in a metal tin held over the fire. We wanted to take one last look at the volcano before we set course on the return journey. This time, we noticed steps going inside it, indicating that scientists had gone some way into the mouth of the volcano to make their observations and had possibly lowered some instruments further down. One of the more adventurous sorts in the group suggested that we go down the steps for a look-see but he was quickly rebuffed. Common consensus upheld that this was adventure enough and it would be stupid to ruin it for a little reckless pleasure.

The volcano appeared changed in the morning, more stoic, less fiery, more majestic, less temperamental, more approachable than and not as enigmatic as the night before. I left Nyiragongo but Nyiragongo refused to leave me. It would be trite to call this experience unforgettable even though it was. I would be stating the obvious if I said that such an adventure is rewarding or educative or simply lots of fun. It was all of these. And it was something more.

Eleven years later, Nyiragongo lives on in me as a place of precarious balance between toil and turmoil, between fear and equanimity, a moment of serenity amidst the grand cycle of upheaval, restoration and resurgence that is life itself. Nyiragongo – a mirror to life in a cauldron of fire.

A Rescue

It was the winter 1987 and I had just converted to the Cheetah (LAMA) helicopter at Bareilly. I was thoroughly enjoying flying the high altitude missions that were coming my way. My seniors in the unit took me along as co-pilot and there was much to learn from them on these missions. On one bright and crisp morning, as we sat sipping hot tea, warming ourselves in the winter sun, contemplating how to spend the rest of our day, we heard the flight commander's scooter coming in our direction. Was he coming with a new mission? Was I to be on it? It would soon be clear.

We were informed that a mountaineer had gone missing in an avalanche near the Gangotri glacier. The crew was to leave immediately for a search and rescue mission and I was to be on it. We were asked to land in Uttarkashi (now in Uttarakhand), where we would be briefed by Col Bajaj, the head of the Nehru Institute of Mountaineering. Col Bajaj had earned his repute as an adventurer, when in 1989, he had skied 1,200 km in 50 days over an uncharted route in Antarctica and been the first Indian to hoist the national flag at the South Pole.

For a helicopter pilot, the opportunity to carry out a rescue and save lives is a special one. I was to fly as co-pilot to Flt Lt AK Sinha, an ace pilot, known as Chinky to those senior to him and Chinky Sir to juniors like me. Chinky Sir was the one who had initiated me into high altitude operations and he was always fun to fly with. Excitedly, adrenalin coursing through my veins, I got into my flying gear and rushed to carry out pre-flight briefing while Chinky Sir got the ground crew to prepare the aircraft for the mission.

Before take-off, we had to check if the winch fitted on the helicopter operated properly since it was very likely that it would be put to use. A winch is essentially a motor driven contraption which reels out a steel cable with a strap and hook attached at one end. When lowered, the person to be rescued has to be hooked to the cable while the pilots hover above and reel in the casualty to safety. In case there is no one on the ground to help in this, an additional rescue crew is taken in the helicopter to be winched down to the casualty. Winching is generally resorted to when there is insufficient place to land the helicopter, typically in the hills, where high altitudes and undulating terrain often allow no place to land.

As part of training for contingency, pilots routinely carry out mock rescues at the airfield. But one rarely gets to do 'live' winching and I, like any young soldier, was looking forward to putting my training to use. We landed in Uttarkashi and proceeded to meet Col Bajaj. We learnt that the missing mountaineer, Minoo Mehta, had been part of a mountaineering expedition team to Mount Satopanth. Mount Satopanth is located in the northern Gangotri glacier at a height of 7,075 meters (23,000 feet) and is the highest summit in the Gangotri group of mountains.

The other members of the mountaineering team had been found but Minoo was still missing. Ground teams along with porters had already been dispatched to conduct searches and they had not reached base camp until nightfall. With communications being what they were in those times, there was no immediate contact with other search and rescue missions.

We took off for the first search mission with Col Bajaj. He carried a huge folded map for reference. He had already told us the likely area of search and kept pointing out the various peaks en-route. Having trained many a mountaineer in this region, he knew the area like the back of his hand. As we climbed past 10,000 feet we had to put on oxygen masks. Clearly, Col Bajaj was used to this rarefied air because he was quite comfortable without a mask. At 15,000 feet, we flew over the general area identified for the search. Even under blazing sunlight, it was biting cold. Encumbered by oxygen masks and goggles that fogged with every breath, we commenced our search for a survivor in the vast expanse of white beneath us. The reflection from the snow and ice at that altitude strains the eye, to say the least. Flying for too long at such altitudes takes its toll, even on seasoned pilots. By the time we were exhausted from the exertion of high altitude flying, the helicopter too gasped for fuel. At this point, the search was called off and we set course to the Uttarkashi helipad to refuel and decide on the next course of action.

As we stood by the helicopter and in deep discussion with Col Bajaj, we were taken aback to see a lady dressed in *salwar kameez* walking towards us. Col Bajaj introduced her as Bachendri Pal, the first Indian woman atop the Everest. Having conquered the Satopanth peak earlier, she had helped Dr Minoo plan for this mountaineering mission. She was a friend and concerned about a fellow mountaineer's safety. We now planned a quick search of the area with Ms Pal on board. She knew the area better than any of us. But the second time too we couldn't spot anyone and returned dejected. With the weather deteriorating in the late afternoon and no more high altitude operation possible, it was decided that we return to base, which was a good two hours of flying away. We told Col Bajaj that we would be back very early the next day so that we could put in more number of missions to search for the man.

The next morning, we got airborne at first light. The going was extremely smooth as early morning flying always is. We were at the helipad at Uttarkashi just about the time that the locals would have got their first cup of morning tea. This time we were equipped to stay the night so that we could continue with the search operation for as long as the weather permitted. When we landed, we were greeted by an elderly man dressed in formals. 'I am Dr Mehta, Minoo's father', he said. I remember thinking how positive he was about finding his son. If he was disturbed, as he was sure to be, he didn't show it at all. He had flown all the way from Pune to Delhi and zipped across in a taxi travelling through the night to be at the helipad by the time we landed. He told us that he had already obtained the requisite permissions to travel in the helicopter for the search and he was ready to leave when we were.

After quick cups of tea for us and fuel for the helicopter, we were climbing away into the blue and crisp sky of the morning. This time we spent as much time as possible over the area of concern and scoured each nook and cranny of the mountain. Dr Mehta kept peering through his binoculars. In every speck and shadow on a mountain of ice, a father will see his missing son. Every now and then, Dr Mehta would spot something in the snow and direct us towards it. As we neared the place, it would turn out to be in vain.

Dr Mehta wore a forlorn look by the time we returned from our futile search. He did not want to join us on the subsequent search flights, he said. We assured him that we would keep trying the whole day. In whatever way we could, we told him not to lose hope. But dejected as we ourselves were, he was the one to surprise us.

'I am very proud of my brave son and I am mentally ready to accept that he is lost forever. I am glad that he went this way', he said.

We continued without the old man through three more missions that day and found him waiting patiently at the helipad for us at the end of each one. At the end of the day, before he returned to Pune, he thanked us profusely for our efforts. There was nothing to be said, no words to say how sorry we were that we couldn't bring back his son. Behind the spirited old man who was willing to accept fate, we knew there was a father devastated at the loss of his only son.

On our part, we had spent three feverish days and nights in search of a man whose face we had never seen, who we knew nothing about. The sense of loss that I felt at never being able to see the missing man made me understand the feeling of duty and the tug of bare humanity that makes helicopter pilots take risks, even put down their own lives sometimes, in order to bring people to safety. It is a fact, sad but true, that rescue missions don't always end with a rescue.

Dr Jal Minocher Mehta, Minoo's father, about whom I found out later, was a Padma Bhushan awardee and a reputed surgeon known for his work in the rehabilitation of people afflicted with leprosy. Minoo's mother was a famous heart surgeon who taught heart surgery at a medical college in Pune. I also learnt that they lived close to my home in Pune and made a mental note to visit them on my next visit there.

A year passed and I was a veteran of many a successful and unsuccessful rescue missions by then. One successful mission that I carried out, almost in the same area where we had searched for Minoo, was that of an Australian mountaineer suffering from HAPO (High Altitude Pulmonary Oedema), a breathing problem known to afflict some people at high altitudes. Flying at the highest permitted operating height, we had perched ourselves on a ledge, one of the skis of the helicopter was hanging in mid-air and the rotors were almost slicing through the packed ice on the other side. Through the side door, we had to haul the man in and take off while his feet were still hanging out. They continued to hang out of the aircraft right until we landed at the helipad at Harsil. When we took off, the Australian seemed to be comatose. Only his laboured breathing assured us that he was still alive. Lo and behold, by the time we landed, he got up on his own and walked out of the helicopter! I was always reminded of Minoo Mehta on these rescue missions that ended in safety for the mountaineer.

Once, while in Pune on leave, I found Dr JM Mehta's number and gave him a call. He told me that the body of his son had been recovered when the snow had melted and the family had given him a snow burial in the mountains. That's how mountaineers are given their last rites, he explained to me. He invited me home to have a cup of tea with his family, an invitation that I readily accepted. As I entered their home, I couldn't have been more surprised – a large gathering of relatives and friends were waiting to meet the 'rescue pilot'. It was embarrassing at first, because rescue pilots are hardly used to such attention, even though it's not something they can't get used to.

Dr Mehta gave a short account of how we had gone about the search for Minoo while a moist-eyed Mrs Mehta went about making sure that there were enough snacks for everyone. At the end, they presented me a suit length. By the time I was asked to say a few words, I was overcome with emotion. All I could say was that we did our best. It was our job to rescue and we tried to, to the best of our ability. I said that I did not think I deserved a gift for doing my job but I would accept out of respect for their family and in remembrance of Minoo. When I was leaving, they handed me another packet – a gift for Chinky sir, the captain of the mission. I had just as much gratitude for what Dr Mehta did for us that day as he had for what we had done for him.

As the years wore on, I kept in touch with Dr Mehta simply because he was delightful company. We used to meet in his small clinic on Main Street in Pune cantonment. One day, at the time when I was then posted in Suratgarh, Rajasthan, a young Corporal came to me in tears. He was from a small village in Maharashtra, and his younger brother had a heart condition which would be fatal without immediate surgery. The nearest medical help available would be in Pune and it would come at a high cost, much too high for this Corporal's family. The heart surgeon, Dr Mrs Mehta flashed through my mind. On an instinct, I wrote a small note to her requesting for help. Along with the note, I sent a small desktop model of a helicopter as a token of gratitude. Hopeful, the young man went on leave and I was posed out of Suratgarh before he could return.

Many years later, a senior Sergeant approached me on one of my visits to an airbase. It turned out this was the same young Corporal from many years ago, who had left with my note for Mrs Mehta. He had a most fascinating story to tell. As soon as he had met Dr Mehta in Pune, he had been sent to a hospital where doctors were already waiting for his brother. They had decided that the boy needed open heart surgery and had proceeded to operate on him in quick time. When the sergeant had offered to pay, the hospital had refused the money saying that the operation had been sponsored by the Mehtas for the family of a military man. The boy's life had been saved and he had gone on to live a full, healthy life.

Little gestures of gratitude, small acts of courage and kind words of reassurance through the years had given an uncommon friendship the power to save a life. And the rescue mission begun on the snowy peaks of Uttarkashi that couldn't save Minoo Mehta had been, in a sense, completed in the saving of another life. Maybe every rescue mission does end in a rescue, if you wait long enough.

Minoo's parents have now joined him in heaven. May their souls rest in peace.

This is why being a helicopter pilot is so different from being an airplane pilot, and why in generality, airplane pilots are open, clear-eyed, buoyant extroverts, and helicopter pilots are brooding introspective anticipators of trouble. They know if something bad has not happened it is about to.

—Harry Reasoner

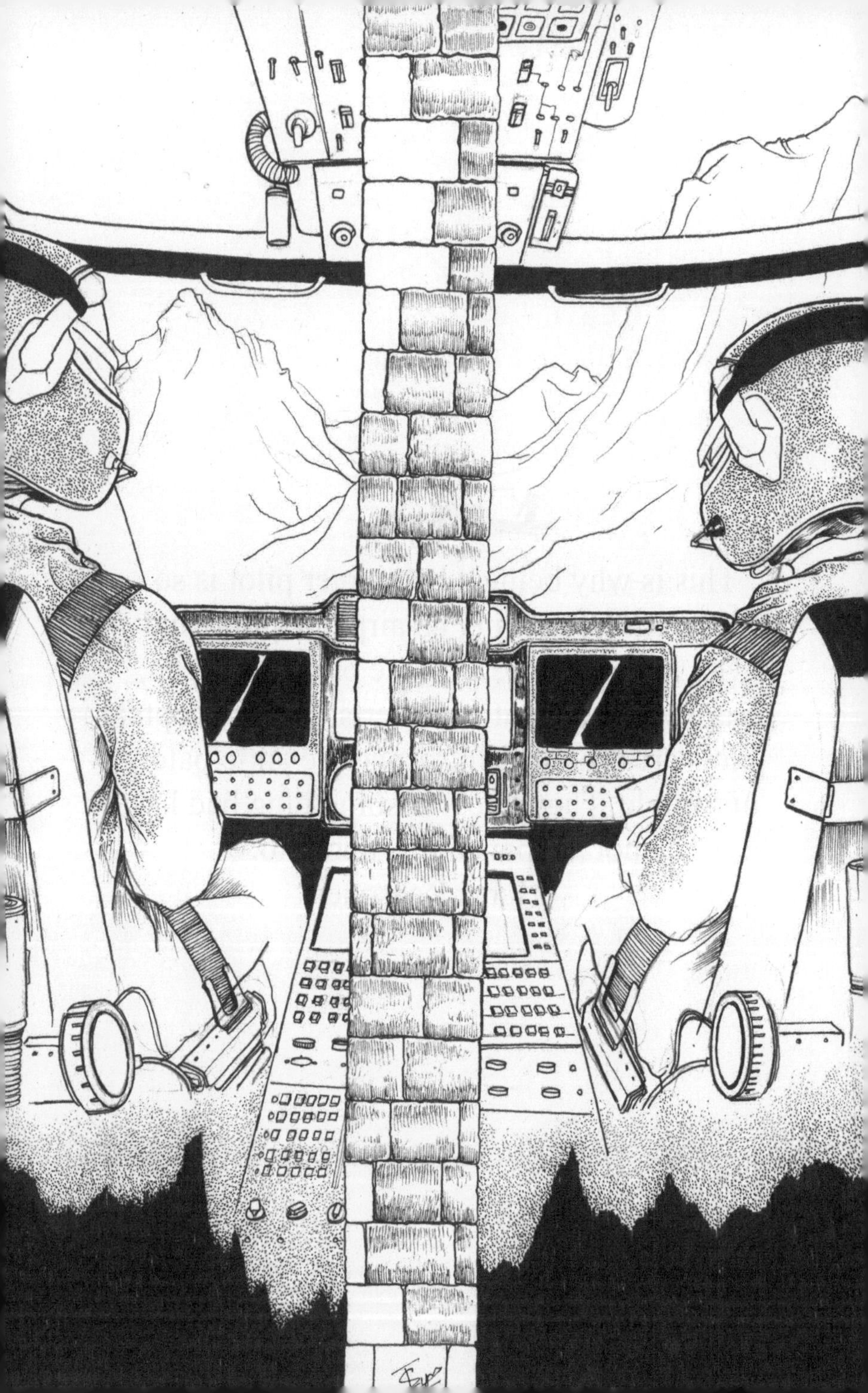

Teach Me Not

Aeroplanes have captains. A captain is responsible for the aircraft and its occupants as also the ground crew who work close to the aeroplane. He or she is also held accountable for the safety of populations on ground in case of a forced or crash landing. When not flying, especially in the Armed Forces, these captains of aircraft are also expected to be captains of men and material. These skills are learnt on the job, in the course of one's service but also come in large part, from each one's personal ethics and attitude. Just like leaders anywhere, captains can be as bad as they can be good. There are examples of great integrity and efficiency but there are also more than a few cases of grossly inefficient captains who discard the rulebook or forget the spirit of flying and flight safety.

The captain of an aircraft flies with a co-pilot. God help the passengers and the aircraft if a disagreement between these two escalates beyond reasonable or professional limits. Even if the aircraft is in top condition and there is no technical malfunction or human error in handling the machine, people in the business of flying know the extent to which human psyche and interpersonal relations affect a pilot's performance in the cockpit. This is a story of a captain and co-pilot team that did not run into disaster but could very easily have.

It was a high altitude sortie and the Cheetah, a small helicopter, was positioned at one of the intermediate refuelling helipads on its way to a far flung region of the central Himalayas. Two senior bureaucrats were to be flown close to the border for an aerial recce. All had gone well so far. The pilots had just finished breakfast when the siren of an approaching motorcade announced the arrival of the passengers.

After the two men had been received and briefed for the flight, the assistant to one of the bureaucrats took the captain aside. Officially, he wasn't supposed to fly but he didn't want to miss the chance to fly so close to the border, he said. He said that he would simply 'tag along' and 'take a look'. The captain agreed immediately. He wasn't going to run the risk of annoying a senior bureaucrat, not even his assistant. After all, it augurs well for professional progress if all the people in power and their support staff are duly humoured as and when one has the good fortune of crossing their hallowed paths.

The captain's pandering to bureaucracy didn't make the co-pilot happy however. He had calculated the fuel for the mission based on the fact that there would be only two passengers. With one extra passenger, he foresaw that the aircraft would have difficulty climbing to the altitude required. Considering the high altitude landing planned after the recce, the aircraft would be at the limits of its power margin during the landing as well. But there was no time to worry. The captain had already strapped up and was getting ready to start. The co-pilot decided to hold his silence. Voicing his concern in the presence of the VIP passengers could be mistaken to be an overreach of his authority. Besides, it would embarrass, if not offend the captain.

The co-pilot waited for the engines to start. Over the intercom, under the din of the rotors, he conveyed his inhibitions to the captain. He was only doing his job, he thought. If the captain was alerted, he could still take corrective action. But the captain simply acknowledged his argument against the additional passenger, raised an eyebrow and initiated take-off. He had a very worried co-pilot beside him now and conversation between them ceased for some time.

At 10,000 feet, oxygen masks became necessary and the aircraft showed the first signs of distress. Climbing beyond 15,000 feet, the machine became sluggish even with maximum power. The captain was desperate to get to the height from where he could show his important guests a view of the Manasarovar lake. It may have been God's mercy or the captain's sheer will power that the helicopter managed to climb to the required height that day. After only a fleeting glimpse of the magnificent sight across the mountain peaks, the machine couldn't withstand the stress anymore and descent had to be carried out immediately. As was to be expected, the important guests were not very pleased about this.

The co-pilot was still on tenterhooks because the landing was to be carried out at a forward base situated at about 12,000 feet. With the correct weight configuration, the helicopter would have had adequate reserve power and landing there would have been a piece of cake. But this helicopter was loaded to the limit. The co-pilot couldn't stop himself from cautioning the captain about the landing. The captain, being senior to the co-pilot, wasn't amused to receive advice from his co-pilot a second time.

'Do you know that I have flown in this area as much as you have flown in your entire flying career?' he said. 'Don't teach me how to fly. You should be trying to learn something instead!'

Amidst all this, the aircraft was on its final approach for landing. The co-pilot was quiet. Despite the fact that the helicopter was not low enough on approach, he said nothing to the captain. The captain struggled to put the machine down and barely averted a crash when the helicopter ran out of power during the final part of the landing. Luckily the guests were too busy with the rest of their official schedule and they sped off for their meeting soon after landing.

'See how I am sweating after the landing. And the temperature here is just about freezing!' said the captain to the co-pilot. The co-pilot remained silent.

'Why didn't you tell me that we were very high on approach? That was more crash than landing!' the captain joked nervously.

Grabbing the chance that he was waiting for, the co-pilot quietly said, 'I was only trying to learn, Sir.'

A few years later, a crash was reported from the North East. The enquiry revealed that the main reason for the crash was that the captain and his co-pilot weren't on talking terms. The captain had poked fun at the co-pilot at a social event. This had not gone down kindly and a cold war between the two men had spilled over into their cockpit. The co-pilot had said nothing to the captain during a sortie, thanks to which they had crash landed and required a rescue crew to free them from the wreckage.

Fortunately for me, I wasn't the captain or the co-pilot in these stories. I saw the damage first hand because I was on the rescue team.

Scientists tell us that the fastest animal in
the world, with a speed of 120 mph, is
a cow dropped out of a helicopter.
—Dave Barry

Tickles

Only another forty kilometres, I tell myself. I have had a rough day travelling solo in my rickety old car, which has taken umpteen opportunities to remind me that she can give up on me anytime she wants, and without notice. She is the reason for this delay and I have been forced to undertake this last part of my journey through dense jungle by night. As I drive through the village at the edge of the forest at last light, the winter fog is settling in. Smoke from small fires outside the hutments hangs just above the earth's surface. For a lone traveller away from home, faced with a jungle crossing after dark, the village reminds me of all the things that are piteously out of reach and intensely desired at the moment – a warm room, the voices of people, a hot dinner and a bed.

I must have travelled about 15 minutes on the winding road through the forest when my rickety decides to sputter and stall. Just the outcome I was dreading all evening, I curse aloud. It is but small mercies that I have a torch with me. *Fauji* preparedness stands me in good stead yet again. I look under the bonnet to see what is wrong. My fuel pipe has leaked and I am seeing the last drops of fuel in a sordid pool on the ground.

What are my options, I ask myself. Not many, comes the answer. There is not a soul, not a moving light in any direction. The howling of hyenas underlines the eeriness of my situation. Even the crickets seem to chirp with foreboding. Trying to stay calm, I try not to think too far ahead and focus on what I can do. I can stay in the car and wait for someone to come by or I can trudge back to the village for help. I wonder how often people cross this jungle by night and if they are villagers on foot, they may not be able to help with a cracked fuel pipe anyway. So I decide on the latter course of action. I hope to run into some help as I head back to the village on foot.

In the dark, somewhere in the jungle, what is the probability that I will cross paths with the miniscule percentage of mankind that is also crossing this jungle on this very night? The statistics are grim. I pick up my water bottle, jacket, a packet of biscuits and brace myself for the unknown. What you plan is holiday, what you don't is adventure. I can't remember where I've heard that line but it is quite apt for the circumstances, even if not in the least bit comforting. Unannounced adventures are most unwelcome!

I don't know how far I have been walking. I have been listening for sounds of man and beast, for a rustle of leaves, watching for pairs of eyes watching me from behind some dark bush or tree. And when I spot two fiery red eyes staring at me, I do exactly what I would have done if I hadn't been watching out for them. I jump out of my skin! How peculiar is fear! I tell myself not to panic, even though all I can think of is to turn around and run. At that instant, when I don't know whether to expect a growl, a roar, a snarl or snort, I hear a whimper. A ball of fluff with a wagging tail reveals itself. Under my flashlight, I imagine I see in his eyes, the same fear that I had in mine moments ago. He seems to be a domesticated dog, used to being around people. I inch closer now. Softly whistling, I call out to him. 'Sweetie! Come. Come here!'

The fellow gets up reluctantly. He limps towards me. Maybe he followed a cat or vehicle and lost his way in the jungle. Maybe he's terrified of the hyenas, not sure if he should come out and walk with me or hide in the relative safety of the bush. Really, his choices are not much different from mine. I walk on, calling him to come with me. I think he has decided to stay and I carry on by myself. After a few minutes, something soft and wet tickles my hand. I yelp and the little dog yelps in return. Am I glad to see him again! He has run off on hearing me shout, probably scared away by my reaction. I call out to him. I don't know about him but I need the company. He follows me this time, from a safe distance. I whistle and call him closer. After a few minutes of walking like strangers, he circles my toes. I squat to give him a pat and offer him a biscuit – an offer of friendship. He gobbles it and asks for more. The hungry little thing! I have a name for him and I tell him. I tell him I will call him Tickles. He accepts with a woof and a lick. The rite of comradeship is now complete. We trudge along, companions on the same mission.

It will be at least an hour's walk before we reach the village, if we are walking in the right direction, that is. The conversation with Tickles eases my worry of the unknown and I decide to enjoy the starlit walk through the jungle as best as I can. How many times in life does one get stranded in the middle of a jungle on a starlit night and find a fluffy white dog for company? I ask Tickles where he lives, how he got the limp. I ask him about the people in his family, his favourite food. I ask him if it is his first time alone in the jungle. Tickles responds in yelps and wags and an occasional jump and lick. He follows close by my heels sometimes. At other times, he goes up ahead, sniffs the path and comes back to me as if to report that he has verified it to be safe to proceed. At some point during the walk, I start narrating to Tickles, the story of my life and end sharing some things that I haven't told even my closest friends. Tickles is a patient listener.

After a while, he runs on ahead, sniffs around the trees and lingers there for a while. Is he bored of my stories? I wonder. I decide to keep quiet for a while for fear that I may lose my companion to my incessant chattering. I feel so much safer in his company. I continue in silence a few steps ahead waiting to see if Tickles will follow me and hoping that he does. Suddenly, he yelps, runs towards me and wraps himself around my legs. I hear a rustle in the bushes ahead. Out rushes a young pig (wild boar would be more appropriate!) and scurries across our path squealing in panic. A short while later a pack of hounds follows. Hyenas or wolves? I will never know. The cat and mouse game of the jungle is on. I hope and pray that we don't come across the bigger game. In this case, it is more likely that jungle life will look upon us as game!

We don't. The rest of the journey is uneventful. We walk close to each other until we see village lights in the distance. With every step we take, Tickles jumps higher and higher in excitement; his version of a jump for he has only one good rear leg. He knows he isn't far from home now. At the edge of the jungle, when we are about to walk clear of the last tall trees and onto the highway, I stop. I want to savour these last moments with my companion. I want to look into his eyes and find a goodbye there. Or a *phir milenge*? But Tickles isn't one for sentimental ceremony. He wags his tail, gives my hand a quick lick and runs off towards the village.

With some friendships, there is no *phir milenge.*

The helicopter appeared so reluctant to fly
forward that we even considered turning the
pilot's seat around and letting it fly backward.
—Igor Sikorsky

Tricked and Taught

It was a check sortie. The pilot under check was a young cadet from the first batch of women pilots to join the IAF. She was to be cleared to captain a small single engine helicopter called the 'Chetak' (Alouette-III).

Those were the days of manual flying, no auto-pilot, just 'eyeball mark-I' for visual reference and 'flying by the seat of the pants' as it was popularly referred to. As the pilot and her instructor approached the hills and the altimeter climbed past 9,000 feet, it was time to wear oxygen masks, remove the headsets and plug in the radio connectors and cords. While the young pilot was putting on her mask, her instructor took over controls and unknown to her, steered the aeroplane 30 degrees from the intended path, a huge deviation from the planned route. When the pilot took back the controls, the journey continued without comment from either side, albeit divergent from the intended direction. After a while the instructor asked the pilot to tell him where they were.

The pilot answered confidently. 'Sir we are approximately three five miles from base and we are flying above Kitcha'.

'Are you sure?' he asked.

His insistence didn't dent her confidence for she had no reason to doubt her direction. 'Yes Sir', she said. She went on to describe the visible landmarks on the ground, locating them on her map. We often see what we expect to see and we corroborate our understanding of the world from our distorted view of it. A common error seen in all walks of life becomes especially dangerous when the stakes are high.

The instructor continued to quiz the pilot further. Now, she probably sensed that she had made a mistake but she still couldn't locate what it was that she had missed. The cadet looked at the instructor quizzically through her mask and visor. The check flight was going horribly wrong now. Until she handed over the controls to her instructor, she maintained that nothing was out of place, she had done all the procedures right, only that she was lost.

'Do you mean that I did something to make you lose your sense of direction?', roared the instructor, sticking to his well-rehearsed act. In the fashion of instructors habituated to flying with men, a free flow of expletives followed.

'I will throw you out of the aircraft since you don't know how to fly!' he said.

'You can take a plane up in the air but you don't know where you are going! Congratulations', he added for effect.

By the end of this tirade, he heard sobbing on the intercom. Tears streamed out of the pilot's mask. It is not that male cadets don't lose their cool or are immune to panic attacks. It is not that young men in control of a flying machine for the first time aren't frightened. Male cadets routinely lose direction when such a trick is played on them too. But instructors who have dealt with many, many new male pilots know the range of reactions that flying evinces in them, especially when they are put in a spot. The instructors of the time weren't used to inducing sobbing and crying in students in the cockpit. Now, this instructor was the one in a spot and didn't know how to respond to this challenge at nine thousand feet!

The sortie continued in silence pushing the poor instructor to his wits end. When the sniffles continued unabated for a while, he put his hands on the controls and said, 'I got the controls!' He immediately set course for base and landed the aircraft without further ado.

'One cannot afford to get emotional while flying', the instructor told the pilot in his debrief. 'This sortie is not to be discussed with anyone', he told her. 'Just say that we came back due to a minor snag in the aircraft. Okay?' He said.

It was possibly a most traumatic and disheartened weekend in the life of the girl. No amount of cajoling by her friends could get her out of her sullen mood. The evening of the following day, there was an insistent knock on the girl's door. When she opened the door, she found she was being visited by the instructor and his wife along with their two small children. The young cadet was ordered to get ready and join them for a drive into town. By the time they reached the club for dinner, the girl was back to being a happy youngster, quite content with the way her weekend had passed! Even though nothing had been said about the disastrous sortie, much had been understood between student and teacher. Both must have finally slept well that night.

There are opinions both for and against instructors resorting to wicked tricks such as these but their intent is never in question. Instructors find ways to test their students, to push them to the brink of what students think they know, to topple them into the abyss of fear where panic lies short at hand, to prepare them for mishaps if they should ever strike them in their careers. It is a horror when you're in the student's seat but many a pilot has silently thanked the good instructor when the tough lesson stands him/her in good stead as a pilot.

When women were first inducted into the IAF as fliers, even though institutional parity between men and women was a given, the organisational infrastructure and its people, both men and women, had to evolve to create real parity on the ground. The crew room culture that pilots held very dear was an all-male culture. Men weren't used to having women in crew rooms. Women weren't used to being in such few numbers in an intensely fraternal workplace that had no precedence of women's successes. Many were new to the demands of operational flying. They had few or no seniors among women who they could look to for advice and the first women fliers had to find new ways to balance flying responsibilities with demands from their families. The provision for separate toilets and appropriate accommodation in the messes had to be taken up by the organisation. Women officers on outstation commitments was another area that had to be worked out. As is true for any organisational change, some people were resistant, some found themselves ill-equipped to deal with the day-to-day challenges it threw up but mostly, everyone coped with it in time and embraced the new workplace dynamics. We have come a long way since then. To create an atmosphere of equal opportunity and equal accountability that takes cognisance of every group's particular needs without giving anyone special privileges is akin to walking a tightrope. We never get to the ideal but that is what we must always aspire to. Kudos to both the men and the women of those early years who bore the teething problems that come with change and worked with dignity and dedication to see an Air Force that is a more equitable organisation today.

The cadet in this story cleared her check sortie not long after this incident and went on to become one of the first women helicopter pilots of the IAF to captain an aircraft. She had a successful career and served the IAF for ten years. During this time, she married a pilot colleague and stayed within the Air Force family even after she hung up her uniform.

A few decades later, the instructor, who was a senior officer by then, was on a civilian flight with his wife. When he heard the captain's name during take-off announcements, the instructor smiled, sprang up from his seat and called cabin crew. On his visiting card, he sent a hand written note to the cockpit. 'Remember me?' he wrote.

A few minutes later, a smart pilot in captain's stripes

walked out to the aisle seat where her old instructor was waiting for her. She shook hands with him warmly. He was used to running into his students everywhere in the Air Force. Women students were likely to be flying for civilian airlines since their period of flying service in the Air Force was only ten years in those days. The instructor was confident that his student would remember him just as he remembered his own flying instructor. He was as thrilled to meet her as she was to meet him, if not more. But he wasn't prepared for what came next. After they shook hands, the pilot asked him to rise from his seat and step into the aisle. Then, in the Indian symbol of surrender and respect, in full view of a flight full of passengers, she bowed and touched the feet of her Guru.

Flying a plane is easy but learning to fly one is not as easy as that. Teaching someone to fly must be even more terrifying. Besides, no student is the same as the next one. God bless the instructors who make good pilots, good pilots!

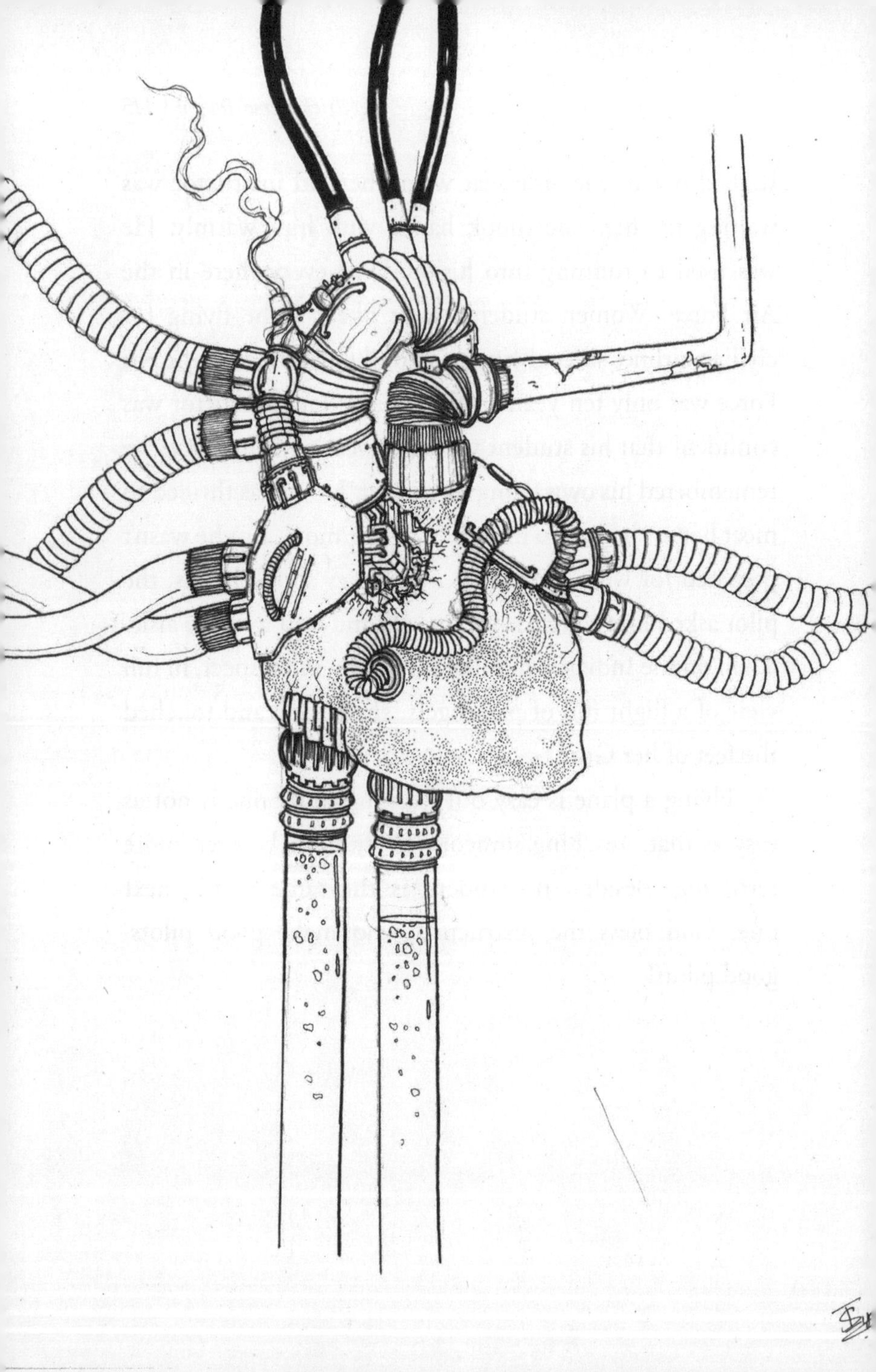

In a Heartbeat

I was at the last stage of the dreaded, annual obstacle course in a pilot's career. At the Military Hospital for my annual medical exam, I had cleared all the examinations by various specialists and the Medical Specialist was the last in line to examine me and clear me for another year of flying. He had been examining me with a stethoscope for a few minutes and I had seen his expression change. Suddenly, he got up and left me lying there in only my underwear and walked out leaving me imagining a million ways in which things could have gone wrong. I was only 31 years young, senior enough to be a supervisor in a flying squadron. My most optimistic guess was that he had gone out for a smoke. Why he needed a smoke just then, I could not reason. After a few minutes, a bunch of doctors entered the room. They seemed excited about something.

As all of them took turns in examining my heart with their stethoscopes, they looked like the first humans to have discovered alien life. Suddenly, they left me and crowded around the specialist's table and got into a discussion in whispers. By this time I was at my wits end, and coughing loudly to attract attention, asked, 'Will anyone please tell me what's wrong?' The medical specialist waited for the rest to troop outside the room before he came to me.

'Do you get palpitations? Do you feel breathless sometimes?' he asked gravely.

'No', I said.

'Do you have any history of heart problems?' he asked.

'No', I said.

'I am sorry. I can't clear you. We have to move you immediately to the Command Hospital at Udhampur. If required they will transfer you to Delhi for further medical care'

As I found out from the medical specialist, I had cardiac arrhythmia – irregular heart beat. My heart missed a beat every now and then, and my heart rate varied – sometimes becoming dangerously fast. The doctors worried that this could lead to a heart attack because of the failure of some valves in my heart.

I had thought I was a fit chap. I played squash every day. The specialist told me that cardiac arrhythmia could happen even if I was drinking too much tea or coffee. But I did not do anything in excess! In any case, that was that. I was asked to pack my bags and report back at the hospital the following day. My medicals were not cleared till I was checked out at the military hospital.

As I went back to the air base on my bike, a thousand thoughts flashed before me. What will happen to my career? Will I be able to fly ever again? Oh, how much will I miss being up in the sky! How will I break the news to family? I had one small child and one was on the way. How will they look after themselves if I have to leave this world sooner than I had expected? What about my parents? Will my wife get the insurance money and will it sustain her for life? What will they check me out for in hospital? How long will I have to spend there? Maybe I won't be able to play my favourite games ever again. I was almost at breaking point as I entered the boundary walls of the base. Instead of heading home, I decided to go to the Station Medicare Centre where we had our own set of doctors, some of who were close friends too.

I was in tears when I related the events of the past few hours to my doctor friend in his office. I told him I was unwilling to go to Udhampur and then get transferred to

Delhi. Could he think of a better way out?

The best of specialists are available at the Central Medical Establishment (CME) in Delhi. He said he would get me an appointment at CME, Delhi and also convince the medical Specialist who had referred me that I be allowed not to go to the Military Hospital at Udhampur.

The last time I had gone to the CME was during my initial medicals for the NDA. It was a gruelling medical exam and all kinds of tests were carried out to ascertain if I was fit for flying duties. They also had measured our limb lengths to ascertain if we were fit enough to fly certain types of fighters. Through all that I had come out clean and in good time. Now I would have to go through another detailed exam. I feared getting caught up with some other problem other than the one that I was perceived to have and be declared unfit for flying. That would definitely mean the end of the road for me.

I went home and broke the news to my wife over lunch. I watered down the problem to a large extent not to make her unduly worried. But by the end of lunch I had her just as worried as I was.

The next evening, I was on my way to Delhi for a very frightening two weeks of my life. After a Sunday spent at my sister's place where she took good care of me, I moved to the CME for the check up early morning on Monday.

I went through the entire gamut of medical tests and was finally in front of Surgeon Commander Jaganayakulu, the senior medical specialist. He looked at me and said, 'Young man, what is wrong with you? You look very fit to me!'

'Thank you! Thank you!' cried my arrhythmic heart. It must have really skipped a beat then. I smiled at him and said with more cheer than I had felt all weekend, 'Sir, I feel very fit too! It is for you to certify it'.

I was put on a 24 hour ECG monitoring machine. I underwent a detailed ECG with a treadmill test thrown in for checking out how my heart behaved under stress. All this done, I reported to Surgeon Commander Jaganayakulu again with all the reports in hand. I sat in front of him with bated breath as he peered over the papers in earnest. Looking up at me, he smiled and said, 'In all probability there is nothing wrong with you. But I need to send you for another test which can only be done in a multi-speciality hospital. I will try and get an appointment for you as soon as I can', he said. Before I walked out of his office he told me, 'If you keep getting tense during your medical tests your blood pressure will shoot like it has now and I will not be able to clear you for flying. So keep calm and get these tests done. It will involve you spending a day in the hospital'.

The doctor got me an appointment for an Electro-

Physiological Study or EPS in short. I was accompanied by my 70-year-old uncle to the hospital. I was to be admitted into the ICU for the procedure. As we went and reported there, we had a funny incident which had me laughing for long after. As we did the paper work and were ready to be escorted to the ICU, the nurse looked at my uncle and holding his hand said, 'Come!' My uncle, in his own jovial way said, 'Not me! This thin guy!' The nurse looked at him disbelievingly and held out her hand to him. 'Come. No more jokes', she said. I intervened and told her that it was really me who needed an admission and not my uncle. The nurse looked at the papers in her hand and after she ascertained the age on the papers, we all burst out laughing.

I had been to an ICU earlier but only as a visitor. Being there as a patient was a different cup of tea. I was in one of the country's best hospitals for critical care. People around me were old and struggling to stay alive. Some of them were on life support and the whole scene was depressing. The smell of disinfectant takes me back to the hospital in Delhi even today. I was wired up and my vital parameters were monitored continuously. Stuck to the bed with all the wires running out of me, the only mobility I had was to operate the electrically operated bed to various angles for comfort. Occasionally, one or the other alarm from the life support systems would go off and the duty nurses and doctors would rush to the patient. Within the first few hours in the ICU I saw two of my fellow patients being wheeled out with their bodies covered in white – not a good feeling at all.

I had brought along a book to read but with all the beeps of the monitors and the constant rush of nurses and doctors around me, all I could do was to observe what was going on around me. I was told that the hospital had a good cafeteria and one could order stuff to eat over the phone, which was within hands reach from my bed. I ordered myself a sandwich and a soup – probably the first time a patient in the ICU had ordered it! And when the boy came to deliver my order, the nurse came along to see who had ordered it. She sternly told me that I was not to have anything before the procedure scheduled for the afternoon and I had to reluctantly send it away.

In the afternoon, I was readied for the procedure. They marked a big plus mark like the cross of Jesus on my chest. Just in case they had to open up on an emergency, they needed to have the markings ready to cut me open, they told me. I was wheeled into the surgery with my heart racing in anticipation of what was to come. In the operation theatre, they spoke with me and asked me to introduce myself. As I replied, I felt a needle prick my upper thigh as local anaesthesia was injected to numb my leg. Doctor

Trehan, the famous heart specialist, then arrived and asked the doctors if all was set. He smiled at me and as an incision was made into my thigh, I felt the blood spurt out of my artery. This done, they cinched it with a clamp and the doctor asked me an absurd question. 'Would you like to listen to music or see a video on the screen?' I said I would like to see what they were doing to me. I watched a wire being put into my thigh and climb into the heart. Dr Trehan asked me if I could feel the wire moving up the blood vessel. I equated it to the change of a clutch wire of a bike and they all laughed at my wit. I suppose my own wit at this stage calmed me down a bit and I relaxed. It was quite something to see my own heart beat on a screen!

'You will now feel your heart racing', the doc said, hovering above me with a syringe in his gloved hand. He pushed in the liquid into my blood vessel and, as soon as he did so, my heart started racing as if I had run the marathon of my life, racing to 220 beats per minute. My chest bounced up and down as if there was something dancing inside me. After some readings were taken, another medicine was injected to slow down the heart beat to as low as 16 beats per minute. This time I felt like I was sinking. May be this is what dying feels like, I thought in those moments. Readings were taken again and my heart was restored to its natural beating. The acceleration and deceleration checks on my heart reminded me of the 'slam checks' that we do when we carry out test of our aircraft for airworthiness. The throttle is opened from idling to maximum in the minimum allowed time of one to two seconds usually. We then note down the time the engine takes to reach the max RPM. A good response is indicative of a healthy engine. There is always a fear of the engine quitting when this slam operation is carried out in the air and therefore we need to be ready with drills to restart the engine if such an eventuality occurs.

My slam check report card was ready by the time I was wheeled into post operative care. Dr Trehan came in rubbing his hands. 'Are you feeling all right?' he asked. 'We have good news for you. Your heart beats the way it does not because of any ailment. You can live a normal life.' The words were sweet honey to my ears and my confidence was immediately restored. The first thing that came to mind was to order the sandwich and soup that I was denied before the procedure!

I was out of the hospital as soon as the wound in my thigh was sewn up and a happy me exited the hospital except for a small limp from the incision, which still hurt a little bit. I had to go back to CME with my reports and get my fitness to fly now. I had meanwhile asked Dr Trehan to speak to the specialist at CME. Confident and beaming, I was in the doctor's chamber the next morning. As I entered, he shook hands with me as if I had won a bout at boxing. He then went on to comment on my medical documents and wrote that I was now fit for flying!

Every time we pilots go for our medical exam, we pray to God that all reports on our tests are within limits. Some of us start living very frugal, disciplined lives for the months preceding the test. Some give up alcohol, others meat, some others go slow on sugar and carbs. We turn into health freaks.

At the end of our medicals, we rejoice and thank the Lord for the remark of the Doctor which says – 'Found medically fit for flying duties. Cleared for all duties of his branch'.

The doctor at CME told me later that my blood pressure may have been abnormally high due to the psychological stress. I promised myself never to get caught by the doctors again. But then the human being is such a complex piece of engineering that something or the other is bound to falter once in a while – one can never tell when one will require the services of a doctor!

The way to fly is to go straight up... Such a machine (the helicopter) will never compete with the aeroplane, though it will have specialised uses, and in these it will surpass the aeroplane. The fact that you can land at your front door is the reason you can't carry heavy loads efficiently.

—Emile Berliner

A Pilot's Privilege

I joined the IAF to become a Fighter Pilot. I trained to be one but fate had something else in store for me. In our batch of thirtyseven pilots, only 5 made it to fighters. Out of the remaining 32 of us, 26 went on to become helicopter pilots while the other six flew transport aircraft. The news, when it came to us, was more than disappointing. While fighter flying was all about high speed, aerial combat and weapon delivery, helicopters in those times were essentially doing more 'humane' tasks like reconnaissance and rescue. Many of us sported long faces for many days after our commissioning. Our instructors told us that all flying was fun. It was the best thing to say to us at the time and it was the last thing we wanted to hear then. We all wanted to be fighter pilots!

The helicopter seemed at first to be a strange machine to fly – it could fly at zero speed, sideways and in reverse too. This was unthinkable for us who had trained on jet aircraft in the initial training phase. So, in moving to helicopters, we had to unlearn 'fixed wing' flying and learn to fly the 'rotary wing'.

The first lesson in helicopter flying is to learn to hover. It appears terribly complex when you begin. The concentration required to keep the helicopter over one spot mentally drains a novice while the continuous operation of controls requiring the use of all limbs has you in physical pain. The more you try to fight with the controls, the more the helicopter flies out of control. It is like horse riding where the horse gauges a rookie at its reigns and does what it likes to do best – to buck and bolt!

Standing on the tarmac, seeing 5-6 helicopters trying to hover used to be hilarious. Like drunk elephants on the dance floor, the machines would buck and wobble seemingly out of control. After a while they would stabilise and appear like perfectly choreographed dancers. (This meant the instructor had taken over the controls.) And then, the madness started all over again.

Over time, we learnt to admire the helicopter for the versatile machine that it is. It can land almost anywhere, carry loads inside as well as slung under its belly, winch up people in distress, take casualties and stretcher patients too. From fire fighting to firing weapons and laying wires, the helicopter is truly an 'all job' machine. Sooner or later, you learn to keep calm, keep your wits about you and be gentle with the controls. 'Treat her like a baby', my instructor used to say. 'Tell yourself to relax and see how she comes in control.' Like riding a bicycle, once we got the mechanics of hovering right, it was easy to hover on every other helicopter that we flew later in life. Soon we didn't have to think about it. It came as naturally as breathing.

When I had gained sufficient experience to captain operational missions, I became responsible for mission accomplishment and safety as also for the performance of my co-pilot, who did the flight plan, briefed the technical crew of the precise requirement of the mission, supervised refuelling at forward bases and reported back to me. From a cadet to a trainee officer to the captain of the aircraft, from a boy who only cared for the thrill of flying and wartime flying at that, I became a man who appreciated the various uses of flying machines and the responsibility that came with it. At 21 years of age, captaining a helicopter must have made me more mature and mentally stronger overnight.

Helicopter flying was my duty but it also became my

foremost passion. Despite the initial disappointment, I, for one, fell in love with the helicopter within a few days into my training. I must confess that I still secretly wished that I could fly something more offensive one day. While helicopters like the Mi-8 and Mi-17 could deliver weapons, they weren't exploited in that role until much later. The IAF was already about to acquire dedicated 'attack' helicopters which were designed for offensive tasks. I would fly them for many years between 1989 and 2000 and then again in 2006-07.

Helicopters are most often deployed in areas where nothing else can reach – in the hills, in disaster struck areas or areas so remote that there is no connectivity by land routes. This became an opportunity to travel to distant places hidden away from all but the most daring adventurers. From the shrines that adorn the distant mountains to the peaks spoken of in mythology to border outposts where there is no one but the valiant soldier guarding our borders, I took every opportunity that came my way. Like many of my pilot friends, I had an insatiable hunger to fly as much as possible. I didn't care for Sundays and holidays. We would carry VIPs – senior officers, bureaucrats, politicians, guests of the state. We would also carry letters to and fro between troops in far flung areas and their families in cities and towns. One day, we would be getting back a wounded or a sick soldier. On another, we would be flying an aircraft filled with flowers and fruits from the places we had landed in. Yet on another, we would be flying with local villagers on board – complete with their livestock too! When our fighter pilot friends were forced to eject, we would rush up into the sky to look for them and get them to safety.

In the summers, we would take off from base at sunrise, operate at altitudes of twenty thousand feet for a few hours, land in snowbound areas and return to the sweltering heat of 40 degrees, all in a matter of hours. In how many professions do you have a chance to take off high above the city and get a breath of the freshest air, all in a day's work?

Once, we were flying in the 'Along sector' of Arunachal Pradesh. After we landed, we were invited by the village head as chief guests for a function in the evening. We managed to get some local bright coloured half jackets which we wore over our shirts and tried to blend with the locals. This seemed to make the villagers very happy. For them, pilots, or *peeloats* as they pronounced it, were very special. *Peeloats* connected their mountainous land to the world beyond. The villagers treated us to their local delicacies. We loved their rice wine and they loved our Rum! After a while we were pulled into the centre of a bunch of dancing women and asked to copy their intricate steps. This caused a ripple of shy, good natured laughter among the local boys. I wished I could return to the village again someday, spend time with the friendly villagers, learn from them about how to live simple and 'wild'. But my call of duty pulled me elsewhere and I could only manage to be to them, a *peeloat.*

Once I landed a VIP in a school ground high in the Himalayas. While he was away on his official visit, I had boys and girls from the school milling about me, wide eyed and full of questions about the helicopter. I answered their questions as best as I could and tried to leave them with more curiosity about flying. I was fascinated by their enthusiasm and good behaviour and whenever I flew over the area, I always remembered to drop toffees for the children. I hope they remember the helicopter and the chocolates. And if they read this and make contact with me, it would make me very happy.

In another instance, I was tasked to evacuate some children from Nainital to a hospital in Lucknow. It was the summer of 1988 and the students had been celebrating the end of their school life when their car went out of control and rolled down the mountain, killing most of the occupants. The delirious cries of the only two survivors – two badly injured boys – still rings in my ears. Sometimes, like one who has lost a dear one, I find myself wondering if one of the young men I pass by on the street, at the airport or on a train, may be one of those boys.

I had been in awe of the pilots who flew in the Siachen glacier, the highest battlefield of the world. When I got an opportunity to fly, albeit a tiny one, in the Siachen glacier, I was thrilled beyond words. I was to carry out a sortie to two of the trickiest helipads in the Siachen glacier. I will never forget the sun burnt, smiling faces of our soldiers in their heavy winter clothing waiting to receive us with cups of hot chocolate. The chocolates, made available in plenty to soldiers at high altitudes, were simply put into hot water to make the concoction. *Kheer* was made using Maggi noodles and the tastemaker that came with the packets of Maggi was used to spice up *daal* and *sabzi.* Helipad markings in the snow were made with coffee powder!

If the rest of us could live like these soldiers for a day or two, off and on, if we could see how they not only smile and survive on so little but also do their duty in some of the harshest conditions, we would return with greater appreciation not only for such soldiers but also of our own duties to our respective professions.

As I moved on to fly bigger and better machines like the Mi-8s and Mi-17s, life flew past at helicopter pace. These were faster machines, could lift heavier loads, fly in worse weather due to the advanced avionics and were much safer to operate since they were twin engined.

When I was commanding a small unit in Mumbai, one of our tasks was to fly to the oil rigs in our old yet reliable Mi-8 helicopters. With no visual reference to fly by and no navigational aids either, it was a challenge. The rigs were located as far as 200 km into the ocean and each landing on those stamp sized helipads on the grossly underpowered Mi-8 taught me a thing or two about flying. Each rig was a small but busy township with all the modern facilities that one could think of. The rigs had a special frequency which could be tuned to for administrative tie-ups. Sometimes, we would radio our breakfast 'order' from the sky and a waiter would be there waiting for us with it when we landed!

Understandably, the crew aboard these rigs did a stressful job in a very dangerous environment and needed to be looked after well. We took the tired crews back to their homes at the end of their period of duty and brought fresh manpower in to continue with the unending task of oil extraction. These people were playing a major role in nation building and we too were proud to be part of this effort.

One of my last stints in operational flying was in the Democratic Republic of Congo. We flew missions to protect and escort other transport helicopters that sustained our troops on ground. Other than that, we also flew what was called 'show of force' missions to dissuade the renegades reversed after four weeks of home and bliss when most of us reunited at Delhi to be hauled back to Pune.

When the NDA special stopped at its scheduled and unscheduled halts, cadets had to get off and head towards the stalls and push carts selling eatables. Cadets on their way home were such a ravenous bunch and the joke went that when the NDA special went on its outward journey, civilian passengers ran away while the shopkeepers downed their shutters.

On one such journey when I was in my fifth term at NDA, we had stepped off the train to buy *biriyani* as usual. We assumed that the halt would be long enough since Jhelum Express was supposed to overtake the NDA special at this point. But we returned with our *biriyani* only to see the red taillight of our train disappearing from view. Most of us had changed into our shorts and vests for the night and were mighty embarrassed to be stranded in that state of undress! For some reason Jhelum express was made to follow our train by the railway authorities that day. It arrived a few minutes later on to the same platform where we stood in our nightclothes.

Fortunately, some of our seniors from NDA who were travelling on the Jhelum spotted us and came to our rescue. One of them went across to the station master and requested him to stop the NDA special train at Ahmednagar which from initiating war. Bullets flew and we flew through this flak safely, thanks to the Almighty and the poor shooting skills of our 'enemy'! This was my first experience of flying in war-like conditions after a long time.

Flying in a foreign land along with the air forces and armies of other nations was a unique experience too. Here we were all 'fighting' on the same side with Pakistanis, Bangladeshis and even mercenary pilots from the Soviet Bloc nations. Often, processes and protocol differed with each country. Since we flew the same machine, it was interesting to watch out for and emulate good practices from one another.

Mi-26, the largest helicopter in the world with an empty weight of 26 tonnes and a maximum weight of 56 tonnes was flown by the Russians in Congo. Each of its 8 blades was 32 metres long and weighed a few tonnes. I happened to be present to watch all the 8 main blades of a Mi-26 being changed by a crew of just three – the captain, co-pilot and an engineer. Back home, we would have taken much more time and employed many times the manpower to get such a job done. But this helicopter was repaired overnight and was flying the next morning! I was awed by this feat. Later I realised that this was because we follow our rule books and laid down procedures to the hilt and do not take any short cuts in our maintenance practices.

The UN mission gave me a chance to visit other African countries in the neighbourhood of Congo. I made many international and local Congolese friends. Living in Africa brought me face to face with the complexity of civil war – a nation with vast resources caught between its own clashing people and hemmed in by vested interests of international players. Africa has been called the Dark Continent and still there is much darkness. The poor, the hungry, the injured and the helpless cannot miss your notice. But living in the 'Dark' continent also makes one see the innate light of humanity in stark contrast with its darkness. Amidst the war, the landscape is beautiful, the people don't forget to smile and one can't help but hope that one day there will be peace in these lands.

Almost everything I know, believe in and value today has been touched and moulded by my life as a helicopter pilot in the Indian Air Force. The pursuit of excellence in any profession must lead everyone to the same lessons, I imagine. In my case, flying has taught me to savour every take off and landing, every view from the cockpit, every operation and every destination, also never to take the machine for granted. It has been a privilege.

I'm always looking for sounds that are pleasing at the time. The sound of a helicopter is really annoying until you're drowning, and it's there to rescue you. Then it sounds like music.

—Tom Waits

Rail Trails

With the exception of the times when I'm flying the plane, I am a pilot who would choose a train journey over air travel any day. Like many a little boy growing up in the 1970s, trains fascinated me then as they do now.

As a toddler, I would drag all my wheeled toys strung to each other in a 'train'. Seeing my enthusiasm, my father soon got me a metal train set that had an engine which could be wound up to pull four bogies on a small circular track. To make it more eventful, I would place a book under the toy tracks. This led to a joyous, planned derailment.

For those of us who grew up in the India of half a century ago, trains were synonymous with holidays. In the days when personal cars and long drives weren't part of middle-class lifestyle, trains gave us agency and mobility. They meant access to family and friends in places whose distance we measured in days and nights of train journey. So Mumbai from Jammu was 2 days and 2 nights. From Dibrugarh to Pune would be 3 days and 3 nights, with a change of trains besides. In the absence of TV and on-demand video, geography textbooks came alive through the windows of train compartments. It was in these that the Western Ghats and the Gangetic plains, rivers and their tributaries, black soil and sedimentary rocks all danced in and out of view while you licked your hands clean of *poori*s and mango pickle.

To be rocked to sleep by a moving train. To wake up and hunt for your slippers in between the suitcases under the seat. To see the sun rise over green fields watched over by scarecrows. To wait for the bridges and the tunnels. To read and re-read the Indian Railways Timetable like a religious text to be cited from memory. To wait for the stations with the best food – *Batata wada* at Igatpuri, *Chikki* from Lonavala and *Chole bhature* at Jallandhar. To wave to the boys playing near the railway tracks, question the ways of God and ask why they got the best deal of all – why they got to live right next to the level crossing! To avoid going to the loo as far as possible. To wonder what would happen if you ever pulled that chain above which it said, 'To stop train, pull chain'. To worry that the engine driver would nod off to sleep in the middle of the night. To dream of saving the train from falling over a broken bridge when he did. Such were the imaginative journeys that accompanied the train journeys of my boyhood!

In the summer vacations, my Army officer father would arrange for the whole family to visit my maternal grandparents who lived in Barsi, a small town about 225 km from Pune. I clearly remember the journeys from Nabha to Pune in a first class compartment which served as our home for the 40 odd hour ride. Daddy would buy a huge block of ice with a large hole right down the middle. This was called silli. He would hire a metal tub to hold the ice, over which a generous quantity of rock salt was sprinkled to ensure that it melted slowly. Into the hole in the ice, which we called the 'fridge', went mangoes, grapes and litchis, bottles of milk and water, sometimes a few bottles of beer for Daddy if he managed to sneak them in. Mummy's unending supply of nimbu-paani and cold coffee was the culinary high point of those journeys.

I would spend hours watching train engines. Just before they pulled the coaches with them, steam engines hissed steam and smoke and their wheels spun fast without traction. It was like watching a bull snorting and clawing his feet before the charge. As a boy, the train engine fascinated me as a thing of great power.

The special thing about the journey to Barsi was the changing to the Barsi light railway at Kurudwadi Junction. The final 21 miles from Kurudwadi to Barsi had 5 halts and took almost 2 hours. The first class compartments in the only first class bogie on the train were still very British in those years. Each compartment had a separate entry from outside along with an attached bathroom, which was several times the size of the toilets found on today's trains. Much to the consternation of my mother, I would insist on taking a shower on this short ride and she would be forced to carry a wet towel outside the rest of the luggage!

The Barsi light railway moved slower than the traffic on the road and stopped at stations that were no more than grassy patches of platform with name boards. On the approach to Barsi, it would cross a road barrier from where our grandparent's home was a stone's throw away. My cousins would wait there to wave out to us, then go home and inform my grandmother that the train was about to reach Barsi. Then the entire family would wait for us to arrive from the station in a tonga!

Another special train was the Deccan Queen between Pune and Mumbai. Started on 1st June 1930, the Deccan Queen was first used to ferry horse racing enthusiasts between the two cities. It went on to become the first superfast train to be drawn on electric traction. I first travelled on the Deccan Queen in 1970. My younger brother and I had a favourite riddle to ask of anyone who cared to humour us – if the Deccan Queen is travelling from Mumbai to Pune at 70 km per hour which side would the smoke go? The answer was that it was an electric train and therefore there would be no smoke! It may seem trite now but it used to be a terribly exciting answer in the days when trains were switching from coal and steam to electricity.

The dining car of the Deccan Queen was as close to fine dining as you got between Pune and Mumbai. Waiters in white uniforms and turbans served omelettes, baked beans on toasts and Dukes' Mangola. As the train climbed the *ghats* and passed through twenty odd tunnels, my father would recount to us the story of the twenty-five thousand workers who lost their lives laying the tracks over these *ghats*. In four hours, the Deccan Queen took you from a bustling, sleepless Mumbai to the sleepy, contented Pune. Today, as the distance between the cities shrinks, as their characters lose their former distinction and merge into one homogenous modern city culture, the train journey too has lost its distinct luxury, its romance and its fine dining. The fact that my Deccan Queen experience can only be memory now makes it all the more coveted somehow.

In 1971, my father was posted to Hyderabad after the war. He took over command of a 'new raising' - a new artillery unit. It was equipped with the massive 130mm 'medium' guns. Twenty guns with their towing vehicles called 'Kraz' along with a host of other equipment like jeeps and trucks arrived by rail in ones and twos, delivered at Hyderabad over a period of three months. From Hyderabad, when the time came to move the unit to Nabha in Punjab, a 'special' train was requisitioned. All men, material and families were to be part of this rail journey and I, then a boy of 8, was excited beyond words at the forthcoming adventure-cum-joy-ride!

I remember accompanying my father to see the rake parked at the special siding at Kacheguda station in Hyderabad. The train had passenger and goods wagons as also flat-top trailer wagons to cart the unit's vehicles. So this movement won't be spotted from air by the enemy, these were covered with camouflage nets. At that time however, I didn't understand why. To us children, camouflage simply seemed to be *de-rigueur* in the army.

In the last few days before we left, the station was abuzz with activity as the train was loaded. A temporary cookhouse was established in tents right on the platform and hot food was served to the men at work on the train.

Naturally, I wanted to be nowhere else but on the platform. I stood for hours and watched as the guns were loaded one by one on to the open wagons positioned at a special ramp. The wagons were then shunted to join the main rake by a small shunting engine. After a week, we finally had our own household packed and loaded on the same train.

The special Army train was like our own cantonment on wheels. There were cook houses for the men and the officers and there was even an all religion prayer room in one of the box wagons. There was a cabin designated as the sick quarters and a doctor travelled in it. An office complete with typewriter, tables and chairs was established for getting routine office jobs done on the move. Some men rode inside the large trucks mounted on the train and I had some exciting moments sitting at the wheel of these vehicles imagining I was driving them.

The first class cabins had the names of the occupants pasted on them and our cabin was called Tiger's Den! Imagine my excitement to find field telephones installed in each cabin of the officers' bogie. To call, one had to rotate the magneto lever keeping the phone in the cradle and wait for the exchange to say, 'Exchange Sir!' The exchange then connected the caller to the number demanded. When my friends and I got to know of this, we started calling each other's cabins through the exchange. For this, we were severely reprimanded and threatened with the withholding of soft-drink privileges. The phone was an essential piece of equipment for command control of the train, we were told. It was used to keep everyone informed of the next halt, to find out if all was well across the length of the train, to decide where and when to stop the train. It couldn't be engaged for children's games. Of course, it was also used to communicate with the cookhouse and order in some snacks or decide the menu for the next meal!

Towards the end of our journey, we planned to halt overnight at Delhi. As a sort of grand finale, bulk tickets for the Rajesh Khanna starrer, *Bawarchi*, had been arranged. When we came back after an enjoyable film, an even more enjoyable surprise awaited us. An entire unused platform of New Delhi railway station had been cordoned off and dinner was laid out for all the officers and men. The high point of the evening was a live band sent by one of the artillery units of the Army in Delhi.

When I write about trains, I cannot but mention the NDA special which took us cadets to our homes and back every six months. This train travelled from Kirkee to New Delhi in about 36 hours. It was a peculiar train because it shed bogies as it went northwards. One bogie was detached at Itarsi for the people going east and into central India while one was detached at Bhopal and so on. The route was

was a good three hours away. The station master, though surprised at this strange request, was nice enough to comply. He ensured that Jhelum express overtook the special at Ahmednagar and we were united with our very worried train mates again. For a while, between the punishments from our *ustaads* who travelled with us to ensure discipline, we became heroes returned from adventure!

In, 1993, no longer a curious boy nor a young cadet but a Squadron Leader posted at Pathankot, I was travelling by the Jhelum express. My wife and I were awaiting the arrival of our first child and I was on my way to Pune to join her there. The Jhelum express, by this time, had become an old and rickety train and had earned itself a pet name – *Jalim* (a Turkish word meaning 'cruel') express. The only improvement perhaps, was the air-conditioned coaches that had replaced first class cabins by this time. On this particular journey, I met a young lady who boarded the train at Ambala. We got chatting and I was happy to find that she was a captain from the Military Nursing Service. We chatted about this, that and the other and I found out much about her training, her background and her aspirations. When the journey ended in Pune, we said our goodbyes and I rushed to meet my good wife who had promptly gone into labour on the day I was to arrive. But our baby took another three days to announce his presence in the world. The third day after my arrival, I reached the ward early in the morning to find that I was a father. As if that wasn't dramatic enough, in true Hindi film style, a nurse in brown uniform came out of the delivery room. She saw me and stopped in her tracks. 'What are you doing here Sir?' she asked. 'I am here for my wife's delivery', I said, wondering where I had seen her.

'Oh, is Pallavi Sathe your wife? Congratulations sir! She has just been delivered of a baby boy', came the response. She shook hands with me and only when I glanced at her name tab did it finally dawn on me that she was the same nurse with whom I travelled on the Jhelum Express only a few days earlier!

Many years later, while I was rummaging through some old trunks belonging to my father-in-law, I discovered a Russian made, electrically driven train set complete with a signalling system and lights. The train was not in working condition and I had to work very hard to get this set going. And when it did, the sheer joy on the face of my young son proved that I had passed on love of the *jhuk-jhuk gaadi* to him.

And... What is More, You'll be a Man, My Son!

In Feb 1981, just short of my 16th birthday, I left home to join the National Defence Academy at Khadakwasla near Pune. Until then, I had been meandering through school, my grades had shown a steady decline due to the numerous distractions of that age and my mother was worried that I wasn't getting anywhere in life. My father echoed her concern but I suspect he believed that I would find my way. A seasoned military man, he hoped I would join his profession of arms. Even his friends and colleagues from the Army encouraged me to do so.

Medicine and engineering were the most socially applauded career choices at the time. To please my mother, I had started studying for the Armed Forces Medical

College entrance exam. Alongside, I also studied for my NDA entrance exam. 'I am doing it just for the experience', I would tell everyone who asked me why I had divided my attention between two widely different streams. I knew why. There was one thing common to both career paths – the uniform!

Getting into the NDA wasn't as easy as I had thought. It still isn't, I can assure you. One had to make it through written elimination tests. Then there was a five day Services Selection Board interview followed by a strict medical examination. By the time one made it to the final merit list, with two hundred and eighty eight names for my course, one couldn't stop gloating about the success ratio of 0.3 per cent.

I remember the day I arrived at the gates of the Academy with a moist eyed mother and a particularly chirpy father in tow. My world was packed into a large trunk as per the list given in the joining instructions. The list included all that was required to survive as cadets from safety pins to socks minus the various uniforms that were to be stitched centrally. One captain, donning the army fatigues was at the gates to receive us, the freshers or 'first termers' as we would be soon called. He was a short, stocky man with a handlebar moustache with a bright yellow name tab that said 'A.S. Rao' in bold embroidered letters which also gave out a sense of what seemed like a dormant temper. The man seemed to suggest a volatile temper and I wasn't exactly happy to see him until he recognised Daddy as one of his instructors from his days at the Indian Military Academy at Dehradun. When he recognised Daddy, Capt Rao smiled and lost some of his otherworldliness.

Daddy introduced me to Capt Rao as the Adjutant of the academy. An adjutant of any army unit is the dynamo who runs almost all affairs of the unit. He is the right hand man of the Commander and executes the Commander's orders. Here, at the NDA wing, he was in-charge of our upbringing, in a manner of speaking.

'Hello Sir', I said, feeling strange to be addressing my father's colleague this way, rather than calling him uncle as I was used to.

'Take care of the youngster', Daddy said to the Captain. I didn't know what 'take care' meant in Rao's books and I hoped it meant the same thing as in mine.

While Daddy and Capt Rao struck up a jolly conversation, Mummy stole a few moments to check with me one last time.

'You really want to join?' she asked.

I smiled and made a face that said, 'Do we have a choice now?'

Among the many detailed instructions about health

and hygiene, I remember her telling me to wash my clothes everyday! How many generations of mothers have snuck in unending and urgent but futile instructions to their 16 year old sons at those gates!

All through boyhood, I had yearned to be grown up so I could one day be an NDA cadet. And now that it was THE day and I was an NDA cadet, I didn't feel grown up at all. When my parents left, I felt small, insecure and vulnerable without them. It struck me that I had, in a sense, left home for ever. From here on, I would only ever go home on leave from service. Although I was used to seeing military life as the son of an Army officer, learning to be an officer was unknown territory. The only comfort in this sea of loneliness was that I was surrounded by many uncertain, bobbing heads like mine.

The next day as we 'fell in' for a head count, I made it a point to stand right in front hoping that Capt Rao would recognise me as one of his. This day, Capt Rao, like every day thereafter, was in a belligerent mood. I tried to catch his eye and I was rather disappointed when he did not show any recognition. In fact, as I made eye contact, he hollered at me, 'Trying to show doubts?' Showing doubts in the NDA jargon meant that one was trying to question authority. 'Get into *murga* position!' he shouted. So there I was, right in front of the line bending down, holding my ears, my arms passing from under my legs looking less like a *murga* and more like a frog about to leap. With my limbs in knots, I couldn't hold the position for long and fell face forward further infuriating the Capt. Thus began the onslaught of physical punishment for the entire lot of us. Twenty minutes felt like hours on the first day and we were all sweaty and caked in mud when we made our way to our dorms. Many of us were so tired that we fell asleep with our canvas shoes on. At around midnight, we were woken up and told to 'fall in' at the grounds next to the barracks. I wondered how Capt Rao could remain angry from morning to night. He asked for a head count because he suspected that some of us had run away after our evening session. In retrospect, I am sure that it was just a ploy. He only wanted to 'sort us out' some more, which in fauji lingo means to take us to task. In PT rig, in the middle of the night, wide eyed and shocked at the choicest expletives that even the most foul-mouthed among us hadn't heard before, we were certainly being 'sorted out'!

Our 'falling in' continued over the first week, at the end of which, we had learnt to front-roll, back-roll, side-roll and contort our bodies in ways that would put gymnasts to shame. Capt Rao must have liked his Sundays because we were allowed some respite on that one day of the week. On Sundays, after the morning games, PT and breakfast, we were allowed to meet our parents at the reception centre. Thanks to the countless bend stretches, like many of my course mates, my arms had swollen up aka Popeye and I had difficulty in bending them even to bring a spoon to my mouth. With my clothes in disarray, my cheeks hollowing out from exhaustion and my hair the typical NDA close-crop, I felt quite ashamed to meet my parents. As I entered with other boys also milling in to meet their folks, my mother took a while to recognise me in the group. Seeing me, she got up with a start.

'See what a week's training has done to our son', cried my mother.

'Exactly', said my father! He held me proudly by my shoulders. 'You ! Enjoying the training?', he remarked. I wasn't sure if he was asking or telling me. I looked from my mother to my father and managed a smile.

'YOUR Capt Rao has been 'sorting us out' ever since the time you told him to!' I grimaced as I said his name.

'This all is to make you physically and mentally tough', Daddy said with no surprise. He had known it would be this way.

My mother was in tears and tongue tied most of the time. And when she broke her silence, she said, 'We can take you back and you can appear for the medical entrance exam and become a doctor.'

After a short meeting, my parents left for Jammu where my father was posted at the time. I would meet them after five months at the end of the first term. All that was left with me was a packet of laddus and chiwda, soon to be devoured by my hungry, new found course mates.

In my memory, the first months at NDA are nothing but physical activity. Convent and public school types, like me, found the degree of physical activity unlike anything that we had imagined. Bend stretches, rolling, star jumps and more bend stretches, rolling, star jumps. Not to mention 'playing' with a medicine ball. This is a heavy-as-a-rock ball, the size of a basketball, that is typically passed around from under the legs and over the shoulders to the next person who passes it back and so on. Although it may sound like a simple enough exercise, it can be very strenuous when it goes on and on. Also introduced was swimming and boxing which were a tough ask for a lot of us. The truism that struck a chord with us in those days was – 'When the going gets tough, the tough get going'.

As weeks turned into months and months into terms, we started enjoying the rigours of training at the academy and learnt to take all obstacles, punishments and celebrations in our stride. One could be excused dinner, excused from a movie, excused a liberty, or excused term privileges. 'Excused' here meant disallowed. But it didn't matter anymore. We understood that we were being prepared for mental and physical strength. Other than basic undergraduate curriculum, we were learning about our armed forces and getting used to the terms like tactics, strategy and operations. We were all heady with youthful vigour, with our growing physical abilities and the responsibilities soon to be entrusted to us.

One year, while on leave during term break, I was driving with my father to Akhnoor from Jammu and onwards towards the border where one of his course mates commanded a brigade. Driving along the countryside, I remarked that the terrain was ideal for tanks and armoured vehicles. As a father today, I look back at my father's amused reaction to my remark as one of pride and wonder at a son sounding 'all grown-up'. That day, Daddy had told me the story of the famous battle of the 'chicken neck' or Chhamb-Jhorian where the Pakistani armour had almost managed to sever the State of J&K from the rest of the country. It was the valiant fighting back of our ground forces and accurate fire of the Air Force which saved the day. It was the first time we had had a '*fauji* to *fauji*' discussion.

The most perdurable gift that the NDA gave us was the group of course mates. Course spirit meant that one could not let down a course mate at any cost, the harshest punishments from the instructors, no matter what. Often, large groups of cadets, sometimes even the whole course would end up getting punished because no one would own up and no one would name the 'criminal'. It is this boyish camaraderie from the days in the Academy that later transforms into the soldierly willingness to lay down one's life for a fellow soldier, a fellow countryman, a fellow human being. It is this that makes the alumni an unbeatable force, both in war and in peace.

My friend, course mate and motivator, Flying Officer MP Anil Kumar wrote a lot about the Academy. In MP's words:

'The cadets at NDA are a microcosmic representation of India. The academy's fundamental objective therefore is to weave this heterogeneous collection into an organic whole with Indianness as its soul ...'

'The camaraderie we foster at the NDA is cast in shared sweat, hunger, torment, fracas, even tomfoolery. Since our ties are born out of enduring hardship together, ours are 24 carat bonds that will easily pass the test of both, time and trials.' One hundred per cent true.

Every year, since I passed out of the NDA, has brought me fresh realisation of what it gave me. Like any good educational institution, the lessons that I learnt then have stood me in good stead for the last four decades.

The NDA was a place where the terms 'manage' and

'sort out' had their own connotations, where the words, 'So you have ideas?' were not encouragement, where 'Liberty' meant permission to visit the city for a jolly time, where horse-riding meant that the horse took you for a ride whether you liked it or not, where you didn't have to be a good swimmer to be thrown into the swimming pool, where you were 'awarded' punishments and where 'feeling funny' was not a laughing matter, where a cadet worth his name could polish off a dozen toasts over a three course breakfast and where scotch eggs traded at the dinner table were worth dying for.

The two pieces of literature that every one of my course mates is sure to know is Rudyard Kipling's poem, 'IF' and the NDA prayer. Whether we remain in uniform or not, these will make our hearts swell, uplift us from desolation, propel us to action and no matter our white hair and weathered limbs, these lines will remind us to give ourselves up to the motto of our great institution – Service Before Self.